GARLAND STUDIES ON

THE ELDERLY
IN AMERICA

edited by

STUART BRUCHEY
UNIVERSITY OF MAINE

A GARLAND SERIES

TELEVISION NEWS AND THE ELDERLY

BROADCAST MANAGERS' ATTITUDES TOWARD OLDER ADULTS

MICHAEL L. HILT

GARLAND PUBLISHING, INC.
NEW YORK & LONDON / 1997

Library of Congress Cataloging-in-Publication Data

Hilt, Michael L., 1959–
    Television news and the elderly : broadcast managers'
attitudes toward older adults / Michael L. Hilt.
        p.   cm. — (Garland studies on the elderly in America)
    Includes bibliographical references and index.
    ISBN 0-8153-2627-0 (alk. paper)
    1. Television broadcasting of news—United States.
2. Television and the aged—United States. 3. Aged in television—
United States. 4. Ageism—United States. I. Title. II. Series.
PN4888.T4H55 1997
070.1'95'0846—dc20   96-36711

Printed on acid-free, 250-year-life paper
Manufactured in the United States of America

To my family for its love and support

Contents

Tables

Tables

Foreword

In her most recent book, *The Fountain of Age,* author Betty Friedan addresses the problem of ageism in American society. Perhaps it is indicative of the scope and the timeliness of this issue that the mother of the women's movement in the United States has now turned her attention to equal treatment for older people. An active 75-year-old, Ms. Friedan has criticized the societal forces that would shuttle her, and her contemporaries, off to the rocking chair. It is through such efforts that public debate and changes in social consciousness emerge.

Social consciousness changes in our society, but it does not change at a steady pace. With recent legal decisions questioning the constitutionality of affirmative action, some might argue that the civil rights movement that emerged in the late 1950s and early 1960s has experienced a step backward in its course of progress. On the other hand, to view the achievements that have been made in this arena, one need only look back over major news events of the past several decades.

The recent death of Carl Stokes, first black mayor of a major American city, may be seen as something of a milepost in the progress of race awareness. One need only contrast the treatment given to early steps toward racial equality in the public press and in the electronic media, which could honestly be characterized as cautious (or not too cautious) alarm, to the fairly mundane reporting that is seen now on a day-to-day basis. An example is the financial crisis the NAACP has found itself in during the past two years. This certainly would have garnered headlines and features stories two or three decades ago; now it is just another news item. Perhaps this is a sign of the acceptance of civil rights organizations into the American mainstream. Their problems are now simply accepted; they're no big deal. The Million Man March on Washington D.C. received considerable attention in the press, but nothing like the attention it would have received had it taken place in, say, 1965 rather than 1995. The passing of Carl Stokes is indicative; one would now be hard pressed to name all the black mayors of major American cities. Thus we can measure progress in the realm of civil rights and changes in public attitudes. In a similar way we might note progress in the women's movement: events and issues that were major controversies a decade or two ago are now taken pretty much in stride.

Such is not the case for public consciousness of ageism. Racist and sexist jokes are out of bounds in terms of political correctness. Bons mots at the expense of the elderly are acceptable. Few personnel managers are unaware of the legal minefields represented by racial or sexual discrimination; age discrimination on the job is still an everyday matter. Everyone knows that corporate downsizing means firing the old guys who've worked their way to the top of the pay scale. Pronouncements from aging organizations are seen as controversial rather than just a matter of current debate. Public outcries for generational equity arise from the basic supposition that the elderly are getting a larger piece of the public pie than to which they are entitled.

In the arena of public debate, a large part of which is represented on the electronic broadcast media, older people are alternately patronized, ignored, or feared. News accounts of Jeanne Calment's recent birthday, which purportedly makes her the longest-lived human, were rife with stereotypical phrases. Little change has been seen since the 1970s, when it was an annual event for the reporters to troop out to the home of Charlie Smith in Bartow County, Florida, to ask him to what he attributed his great age. In Mr. Smith's case, the actual reason for his remarkable longevity was *lying*, he was really 103, not 137, when he died in 1979 (Freeman, 1982). Reporters snigger that Jeanne Calment takes a cigarette and a glass of brandy now and again. Indeed, the stories written about Charlie Smith seemingly could be used for Jeanne Calment, altered to insert a birth date of 1875 and a different name and place of birth. Perhaps the cuteness of these accounts will some day be seen with the same sense of impropriety vis a vis great age that we now view the Rastus in the watermelon patch racial humor of the 1930s.

Johnny Carson's popular "Aunt Blabby" character, a partially-senile battle-axe who'd occasionally take a belt of whiskey from the flask concealed in her walking cane, was quietly retired long before Carson's own retirement a few years ago. This was in response to protests from the Gray Panthers, an advocacy group of older people. Similarly, the muppet "Professor Arid," a college teacher so old and boring that he was actually put to sleep by his own lectures, disappeared from *Sesame Street* early in the 1980s. Thus, there is some evidence of the media being responsive to changing norms, or at least the specter of pressure groups' disapproval. However, there is much progress yet to be made. One study of older characters in television dramatic roles indicates that they are disappearing; rather than project a negative image, producers are opting to portray no image at all (Rubin, 1988).

Viewing the parallels of racism and sexism in contrast to ageism in perspective, one must conclude that we've not come very far at all. *Grumpy Old Men*, a movie hit from a few years ago, now has a sequel that promises to be an equally big box office attraction. We see no one protesting the theme or the title of these films; imagine a feature film entitled, say, "Shiftless, Ignorant Negroes," being released by Hollywood, or, "Dingbat Housewives." This just wouldn't happen in these concluding years of the 20th century.

Ageism has a rich heritage. We were amused to recently discover a feature article in *Life* magazine from 1938: "Old Age -The Old in America Have Become a Political Force & Economic Menace." The unnamed author opines: "As individuals, most old people are pleasant and undemanding. But in today's frightened and uncertain world, the old folks of America have become fearful and insecure. They have banded together to demand Government pensions. By sheer numbers and singleness of purpose, they have become a great political force and grave economic menace." It was pointed out with alarm that fully a fourth of older Americans then received government old-age assistance.

As early as 1971, gerontologist Erdman Palmore from the Duke University Center for the Study of Aging and Human Development, published a study of humor about -- and at the expense of -- older people. He pointed out that we seek to laugh at that which threatens us. He noted that the ancient Greeks, who perhaps even more than the contemporary Americans admired the ideal of youth and beauty, thought that farting jokes were a laugh riot. Sociologist Antonin Obrdlik published a study in 1942, pointing out that one way the Czechs were coping with the German occupation was by making up jokes about them. One need not carry this point too far; our own observation is that there appeared more than three single-spaced pages of O.J. Simpson jokes on the Internet within hours of his acquittal. An example: The good news is that they've finally found and arrested Hitler; the bad news is that the trial is going to be in Los

Angeles. Such jokes are an effort to defend ourselves against perceived threats, as we pointed out in a recent article on the humor associated with death and dying (Thorson, 1993).

Perhaps the reason we see stereotypical accounts -- or no accounts at all -- of the aged in the media is that they are seen as a threat, a threat that is best dealt with by aggressive joking but not serious news analysis. Certainly, most people view the oncoming imbalance of the Social Security trust fund as a major crisis and a threat to our economic future. Few politicians have the stomach to tackle this problem in earnest. Senator Daniel Moynihan has publicly stated that it would be political suicide to attempt to take on this issue seriously. It is fairly obvious that a combination of benefit reductions and tax increases is the only rational way to avert impending disaster. Is this something that appears on the 6:00 p.m. news? Neither station managers nor senators wish to stir up this particular hornet's nest. Perhaps the problem will go away if we ignore it.

Further, it may not just be the aged as a political power block who represents a threat. Perhaps it is the process of aging itself. Like the Greeks who saw indigestion and stomach gas as the antithesis of youthful perfection, we seek to cope with gray hair and crows' feet by joking, "I'm getting so old that I won't buy green bananas." Or, we simply seek to ignore or hide the problem of personal aging in the same way that alarming public policy items are ignored or hidden from the evening news. Armies of plastic surgeons are making fortunes lifting faces and bosoms, transplanting hair, and sucking the fat from beneath the skin of aging individuals. Alzheimer's patient Ronald Reagan still has his hair dyed regularly, as if to beguile his caretakers that he is still youthful and dynamic. The cosmetics industry accounts for billions of dollars worth of annual purchases, all in a vain attempt to cover up what we really look like. How many of use, with the proper application of nostrums and unguents, can *really* look like the *Cosmopolitan* cover girl? Speaking of which, who is the *Cosmopolitan* cover girl? It certainly isn't Betty Friedan.

A serious attempt to cover the aging story in any depth probably will not add many readers to the print media nor viewers to the electronic media. As a nation, we'd prefer to ignore aging -- or try to laugh it off. In this study, Michael Hilt has found that those who decide what news will appear on our television screens have yet to take aging seriously. Is this the result of attitudinal barriers, their own ageism? Indicative of the problem, Dr. Hilt found in his research that many television managers had never really given much thought to aging issues as important public policy programs. Perhaps ignoring an area of public debate is the ultimate insult: older people are so unimportant as to not merit coverage, except in stereotypical, patronizing terms. To say that old people are a threat, as the anonymous author of the *Life* article was brave enough to do back in 1938, has lost political correctness. Maybe the problems will go away. Or, maybe the problems of generational equity, health care expenditures, unfunded pensions, and the ultimate collapse of Social Security will become such glaring issues as to dominate the headlines at the beginning of the coming century.

This may well be the case, and we may well hearken to Michael Hilt's insightful analysis as one of the prophetic studies, the first of its kind, that will be replicated over and over again in the decades to come because it deals with such an important issue.

James A. Thorson
Omaha, Nebraska
April, 1996

REFERENCES

Freeman, J.T. (1982). The old, old, very old Charlie Smith. *The Gerontologist, 22,* 532-536.

Friedan, Betty. (1993). *The fountain of age.* New York: Simon & Schuster.

Obrdlik, Antonin. (1942). Gallows humor - A sociological phenomenon. *American Journal of Sociology, 47,* 709-716.

Palmore, Erdman. (1971). Attitudes toward aging as shown by humor. *The Gerontologist, 11,* 181-186.

Rubin, A.M. (1988). Mass media and aging. In C. Carmichael, C.H. Botan, & R. Hawkins, (Eds.), *Human communication and the aging process.* Prospect Heights, Il: Waveland Press, 155-165.

Thorson, James A. (1993). Did you ever see a hearse go by? Some thoughts on gallows humor. *Journal of American Culture, 16*(2), 17-24.

Preface

Television news has become the public's most important source of information. Older viewers are major consumers of television news. They rely on it for both information and entertainment. They prefer television news over radio, newspapers, and other media. However, information about elderly people and issues of importance to them in television newscasts has been inadequate.

The purpose of this study was to discover the television general managers' and news directors' attitudes toward the elderly and their issues, and to attempt to explain why older adults may not be considered a crucial part of the television news viewing audience.

As the population grows older, the importance of local television news in the lives of the elderly must be considered. The study of the attitudes of broadcasters toward older people will be increasingly relevant.

I would like to thank the members of my dissertation committee: Jim Thorson, Warren Francke, Kent Kirwan, and Chuck Powell. Their guidance was invaluable. I would also like to thank my colleagues in the Department of Communication at the University of Nebraska at Omaha, especially Jeremy Lipschultz, Bob Carlson, and Hugh Cowdin. And a special thank you to Vi Whitsell for her computer assistance.

Most of all, I would like to thank my wife Debbie, and sons Adam and Eric, for giving me the time and encouragement needed to complete this project.

Television News
and the Elderly

I

Introduction

Studies and rating surveys agree that television news has become the public's most important source of information (Bower, 1985; Iyengar & Kinder, 1987; Coulson & Macdonald, 1992). Roper (1989) indicated 66 percent of those surveyed rely on television more than any other medium as their primary source of news. In addition, viewers feel the way television news is presented has improved over the years (Bower, 1985).

STATEMENT OF THE PROBLEM

Elderly people spend more time with television than any other medium (Harris, 1975; Moss & Lawton, 1982) and watch more TV than younger people (Bower, 1973). Older adults spend far more time watching television than reading newspapers, and watch more television than any other age group (Moss & Lawton, 1982; Atkins, Jenkins, & Perkins, 1990-91). While watching television, the older viewer prefers news, documentaries, and public affairs (Steiner, 1963; Davis, 1971; Bower, 1973; Wenner, 1976; Davis, Edwards, Bartel, & Martin, 1976; Korzenny & Neuendorf, 1980; Rubin & Rubin, 1982a; Rubin & Rubin, 1982b; Davis & Westbrook, 1985; Goodman, 1990; Scales, 1996). The older viewers are major consumers of television news, preferring television news over other media (Doolittle, 1979) because they view it as a way to become aware of current events rather than as a diversion (Davis & Davis, 1985).

However, information about elderly people and issues of importance to them in television newscasts has been inadequate (Hess, 1974). Hess wrote that the media have missed "a truly big story" (1974, p.84). The media have been charged with failing to capture the reality of being old in America, and with creating and reinforcing negative stereotypes about old people (Schramm, 1969; Gantz, Gartenberg, & Rainbow, 1980; Bramlett-Soloman & Wilson, 1989; Markson, Pratt, & Taylor, 1989). Although it is 25 years old, Wilbur Schramm's research (1969) still rings true: the media have overlooked the very fact of the emergence of elderly people as a major segment of the population.

The older population in the United States is increasing dramatically (Barrow, 1989). Census projections show that by the year 2040, the nation could have more people over age 65 than under age 21, and more than one in four Americans will be 65 or older (Usdansky, 1992). In the 1990 census figures adults 65 and over accounted for one out of eight Americans, compared to one in 25 at the beginning of this century. Furthermore, the over-85 age group represents the fastest-growing segment of the population (Dychtwald & Flower, 1989). Television news executives should consider this growing segment of the audience when contemplating programming decisions (Hilt, 1992).

Previous studies of elderly persons have examined use of all media (newspapers, radio, television) by older adults or television entertainment programs' depiction of them. Atchley (1991) wrote that it is difficult to generalize about the way aging is portrayed by television, because it is such a varied and complex medium. He found little research had been conducted into the portrayal of older adults in television news. Another issue that has been overlooked is the television managers' attitudes toward elderly people -- a significant part of the viewing audience.

Television news shows a tendency to be biased toward reporting events, especially catastrophes, rather than covering issues (Saltzman, 1979). Atchley (1991) wrote that network news, local news, and documentaries thrive on sensationalism. There is nothing sensational about people who successfully cope with everyday life. So, according to Atchley, those older people who are given attention in the news are those with "a problem that can be a springboard for human interest or commentary" (1991, p.289). Aging and its inherent problems occur over time and usually are not associated with the simple situations which are characteristic of television news programming. The media also are accused of showing a bias against elderly people by failing to report information about aging (Powell & Williamson, 1985), leaving some elderly feeling socially insignificant and powerless.

There have been calls for research into the needs of media personnel for information about the aged (Atkin, 1976). Barton and Schreiber (1978) called for an examination of the internal structures and functions of media organizations as they relate to aging. Such research would reveal how aging as a content topic and as a social issue among staff members is dealt with at critical stages of the mass communication process. More than ten years ago Rubin (1982) listed six areas of inquiry for future research into television and aging: 1) continue examination and development of functional life-position indicators as alternatives to chronological age; 2) continue examination of the interactive communication needs and media uses of aging and aged persons and how certain media behaviors gratify these needs; 3) research the area of non-television media and aging; 4) empirical evidence to establish the extent of television's social influence; 5) examine the uses which older people can make of the evolving new technologies and the impact of these technologies on television programming and other media content; 6) examine the policies and procedures of television in monitoring their presentations of aging-related issues and portrayals.

SIGNIFICANCE OF THE STUDY

The present study will attempt to discover the television general managers' and news directors' attitudes toward the elderly and their issues, and try to explain why older adults may not be considered a crucial part of the television news viewing audience.

Television general managers and news directors, either through a conscious decision or an involuntary act, follow the desires of society put forth in the social gerontology disengagement theory. The theory is a useful framework for the examination of attitudes about older people.

The disengagement theory (Cumming & Henry, 1961; Young, 1979; Passuth & Bengtson, 1988) argues that society and the elderly are mutually obliged to withdraw from each other. The authors of this theory, Elaine Cumming and William Henry, maintained that the process is functional to both society and the individual; it enables society to make room for more efficient young people while, at the same time, allowing the elderly time to prepare for their eventual total withdrawal from social life -- death. Cumming and Henry argued that the disengagement theory should actually be considered an interpersonal communication theory, since mass communication researchers say television serves as a substitute for interpersonal contacts among elderly people: "In television, especially, the image which is presented makes available nuances of appearance and gesture to which ordinary social perception is attentive and to which interaction is cued" (Horton & Wohl, 1986, p. 185).

The theory of disengagement has generated much criticism. Barrow (1989) contended that one might just as well speak of society excluding the elderly as disengaging them; perhaps the withdrawal of older people is a reaction to a society that excludes them. It may be that older adults are being pushed out of society, and television contributes to the disengagement by not showing or speaking about elderly people in its programs. Thorson (1995) wrote that the disengagement theory, like many studies of the aged, tended to lump all older adults into one group and not allow for individual differences.   Whitmore (1995) concluded that there is little knowledge about the portrayal of older people by the news media, and that television news tends to treat the elderly in a superficial manner by focusing on the extreme.

For this reason, the present study is important, and should interest gerontologists, mass communication researchers, and television news executives alike.

Gerontologists should take note of the gap in the literature, and the lack of information concerning the broadcast managers' attitudes toward elderly people. These attitudes may impact the overall pattern of behavior by the broadcast managers toward elderly people (Ajzen & Fishbein, 1980), and thus impact what is seen by the general public on television.

Mass communication researchers should be interested in any study that may confirm the use of television as a way to possibly eliminate disengagement effects (Carmichael, 1976).

Television news executives should be interested because the elderly audience is growing. Recent research conducted for the ABC Television Network found that viewers age fifty and older were significantly more interested in news than younger generations (Wurtzel, 1992). Thanks to health care improvements, people in their 60s and older are living longer, and have more disposable income than ever before (Lieberman & McCray, 1994). Americans fifty years of age and older control half of this country's discretionary income and 77 percent of its assets (Grey Advertising, 1988), and the 65-74 cohort has the highest percentage of discretionary income of any ten-year cohort (Wolfe, 1987). While all of this is happening, news has become a major profit center at local stations (Wicks, 1989). However, broadcast news, entertainment, and advertising have been geared toward younger adults, the so-called money makers who buy goods. Over the years the television networks have cancelled programs which attracted an older viewing audience, such as *Red Skelton* and *Lawrence Welk*. In a more recent example, NBC targeted older viewers in the 1980s with series such as *Golden Girls*, but "cancelled those programs in an effort to attract a younger audience" (Head, Sterling, & Schofield, 1994, p. 308).

Broadcasting is no different than any other business. It should serve consumers without resorting to ageist stereotypes and biases. Unless the television industry gives attention to older Americans, it may alienate an already large and constantly growing segment of viewers.

II

Review of Literature

Research into network television news divisions found that the organizational structure was the most important factor in the framing, selection, and production of news (Epstein, 1973). Epstein concluded that much of how news was gathered, processed, and delivered at the network level was related to organizational needs and constraints. Gans (1979) found that journalists, whether in broadcasting or print, share messages about society with their audience. Goedkoop (1988) found the same could be said for journalists at the local television level.

The general manager is the person in charge of the local television station -- either through ownership of the station or by appointment from the station's board of directors. The general manager is the person who would hire the news director. The news director is the key individual in any local news operation (Goedkoop, 1988). In most newsrooms the news director is responsible for managerial duties such as hiring and firing, purchasing equipment and budgeting, and setting newsroom policy. There is a growing managerial role on the part of news directors that is related to the increasing role of the news department in the finances and programming of television stations (Stone, 1988; Quarderer & Stone, 1989a; Quarderer & Stone, 1989b). However, since local news can take several hours of air time per day, major decisions involving the newscasts are made in concert between the general manager and news director, and possibly managers from other station departments.

The news director is ultimately responsible for the news coverage (Fang, 1985). The news director controls the content of newscasts through hiring newsroom employees with similar views, and setting newsroom policy. The news director would hire the assignment editor -- the person in charge of the day-to-day coverage of news. This person selects and assigns the stories to be covered by the newsroom employees on a given day. These decisions are based on the events of the day, such as government meetings and crime reports, and policies established by station management. For example, the airing of a health report in every six o'clock newscast is a decision made at the highest levels within the station. Factors in making such a decision would include the cost of the report and the type of audience the station hopes to attract. When a news department decision is made that will impact the budget or the ratings, the general manager and the news director are always involved.

Lipschultz and Hilt (1992) provided a demographic portrait of broadcast general managers and news directors. General managers' mean average age was about seven years older than the news directors (44 to 37). Both groups were predominantly white male, and both groups were likely to be married with at least one child. It was most often the case for both groups that their fathers had been manager/professionals and their mothers had been homemakers.

TELEVISION USE BY ELDERLY PEOPLE

There is some indication that elderly people spend much of their day watching television (Nussbaum, Thompson, & Robinson, 1989). Elderly people watch more television than any other age group of viewers, and they tend to watch news and informational shows rather than pure entertainment. Numerous studies show that use of the media increases during middle age through the retirement years (Dimmick, McCain, & Bolton, 1979). More than thirty years ago, Glick and Levy (1962) referred to the elderly as "embracers" of television; they seem to have a "close identification with television, a rather indiscriminating and accepting attitude toward it, and usually (make) great use of the medium." Frequency of television use and total viewing time increases with age up to about 69 years, before showing a slight decline (Harris, 1975). People 55 years and over watch an average of seven more hours of television per week than younger adults (Nielsen, 1975). Nielsen found elderly people watch between 30 and 35 hours of TV per week.

Bower's study (1973) found that "older persons spend more of their time watching the news." His 55-year-and-over group had the highest rate of any age group for viewing "news" and "information and public affairs." Steiner (1963) had reported similar findings ten years previously. Steiner found people 55 to 64 years watched 16.4 television news and information programs per week, and those 65 years and older watched 22.4 programs per week. These were the two largest age groups for viewing television news and information programming.

Doolittle (1979) separated an older cohort into three subgroups: younger seniors (48 to 66 years); old seniors (67 to 74 years); and older seniors (75 to 93 years). Of the three subgroups, television news usage was the highest for old seniors (67 to 74 years). Overall, these respondents gave the highest credibility to television.

In a study conducted by Kent and Rush (1976), 99 percent of the elderly persons surveyed said they watched television news. This heavy use of television news remained fourteen years later, when Goodman (1990) found that older men and women favored television for their national news and information, but preferred newspapers for local news.

Several explanations have been given for age-related trends in media use. Comstock and his colleagues (1978) grouped the elderly along with the poor and ethnic minorities into the category of "disadvantaged." They said this group depends on television more than any other news medium for knowledge and information. The elderly audience's use of the broadcast medium may be related to the ease with which it can be received. Television, beyond the cost of the set, costs less than newspapers and magazines. In addition, failing eyesight can make reading difficult or impossible (Chaffee & Wilson, 1975).

Another reason given for increased use of the media by elderly people is that television and newspapers have become substitutes for interpersonal contacts (Davis, 1971; Graney & Graney, 1974; Graney, 1975; Rubin & Rubin, 1982b). Because of loneliness and disengagement, older adults turn to mass media for their information about the outside world (Schramm, 1969; Hess, 1974; Atkin, 1976; Powell & Williamson, 1985). The disengagement theory of aging suggests that as people grow older they are likely to show less interest in society's problems (Cassata, 1985). Cassata found that television news allows them to feel connected to the world, and the news also supplies them with the information required for "adaptive functioning". This finding has been offered as evidence to challenge the disengagement hypothesis. People disengaged from society would not seem likely to be interested in television news, but elderly people show high interest. Atkin (1976) suggested that the preference for news and information in television viewing is a direct attempt to compensate for the stable and unexciting world of older adults. Schramm (1969) interpreted this as their way of keeping up with society rather than a means of disengagement. He wrote that older people use television to keep in touch, combat progressive disengagement, and maintain a sense of belonging to society. Lowenthal and Boler (1965) found those aged adults who voluntarily disengaged from their social activities decreased use of media, and those involuntarily disengaged increased their use. Kubey (1981) found that television may help substitute for the information network that existed when the individual went out into the community to work. The increased leisure time that accompanies retirement may account for some of the higher consumption rates of television news by elderly people. The substitution theory has been offered as an alternative to the disengagement theory. The substitution theory of aging holds that older persons will tend to substitute mass media communication for interpersonal communication when the latter is unavailable, or extremely difficult to accomplish (Bliese, 1982).

TELEVISION PORTRAYAL OF ELDERLY PEOPLE

Considerable research has been conducted in two theoretical fields relative to the portrayal of elderly people in the mass media and specifically on television. Two primary hypotheses about media effects have emerged from this research.

First, the cultivation theory holds that people watching television acquire a view of the real world shaped by the televised content they view. Gerbner (1969) noted that, if elderly people are portrayed on television as incompetent, viewers may begin to think that is true. Signorielli & Gerbner's (1978) prime-time television analysis of more than 9000 TV characters found that elderly people were not often represented. When they were, they often had problems and were reliant on younger people for help (Northcott, 1975); were more likely to be villains than heroes (Aronoff, 1974); or, simply were portrayed in a negative light (Davis & Kubey, 1982). More recent research (Bell, 1992) found that negative stereotypes of elderly people in prime-time television have been replaced by more positive stereotypes. However, Bell added that these portrayals should mirror the demographics of the country, not just in the number of older people shown on television, but also in gender, race, class, marital and health status. Gerbner (1993) found in a study of women and minorities on television that older people are greatly underrepresented, and seem to be declining instead of increasing as in real life. Cultivation theorists would say that heavy television viewers may think that few people are elderly and that elderly persons were of less consequence since they were not seen.

Other research in the area of television's portrayal of elderly people includes Saturday morning cartoons (Levinson, 1973; Bishop & Krause, 1984; Powers, 1992), game shows (Danowski, 1975), television commercials (Francher, 1973; Schreiber & Boyd, 1980; Hiemstra, Goodman, Middlemiss, Vosco, & Ziegler, 1983; Swayne & Greco, 1987), fictional television (Greenberg, Korzenny, & Atkin, 1979), prime-time television (Petersen, 1973; Dail, 1988; Cassata & Irwin, 1989) and soap operas (Ramsdell, 1973; Downing, 1974; Barton, 1977; Cassata, Anderson, & Skill, 1980; Cassata, Anderson, & Skill, 1983; Elliott, 1984).

A second hypothesis about media effects involves agenda setting, which suggests the media will influence the way people think by focusing viewers' attention on specific issues (Nussbaum, Thompson, & Robinson, 1989). The media set the agenda for the audience by emphasizing certain topics and by slighting other issues through omission. Agenda setting can enter television news programs through event bias, i.e., television newscasts tend to report events (e.g., fires, car accidents) rather than non-event issues (e.g., plight of elderly people, starvation). Television can reinforce stereotypical attitudes toward elderly people (Gerbner, Gross, Signorielli, & Morgan, 1980). Lonely elderly viewers in one study showed greater interest in viewing negative rather than positive portrayals, whereas non-lonely subjects exhibited the opposite preference (Mares & Cantor, 1992). Results of a national survey published in *Parade* magazine (Clements, 1993) show that more than half of the respondents feel the elderly are portrayed favorably in television (62 percent), movies (59 percent), and advertising (55 percent). One respondent who disagreed said that the average person who doesn't have close contact with the elderly and only sees them through the media would get an incorrect perspective. "This may be one reason why many people treat the elderly as children, as if someone else would be better at deciding what's best for them" (Clements, 1993, p. 5).

Many Americans fear growing old. Friedan (1993) placed much of the blame for this fear of aging with the media. Although studies of television's portrayal of elderly people do not conclude that the elderly are inaccurately depicted, very few conclude that the portrayals are positive. Also, although many older persons spend substantial time with TV and like to watch it, such older viewers have not been a significant factor in commercial television programming decisions (Carmichael, 1976; Carmichael, Botan, & Hawkins, 1988). Programming decisions are often based on the number of people watching a particular show -- the ratings. If the ratings are low, or if the advertisers do not buy commercial time because they do not want to market their product to the type of people who watch that program, the show soon will be off the air. The ABC

Television network, along with the other major television networks (CBS, NBC, and FOX), considers its core viewers to be adults in the 18 to 49 age group, teenagers, and children ages two to eleven (Wurtzel, 1992). According to Rubin (1988), programmers and advertisers typically have ignored the needs and wishes of over 20 percent of the population, those past the age of 54. In fact, television advertisers control what is seen. Elderly persons do not feel television commercials give an accurate picture of older people (Harris, 1981). Research has found a positive relationship between television orientation and concern for one's personal and financial well-being (Rahtz, Sirgy, & Meadow, 1989). This might be useful in helping advertisers select the appeal which would be most effective among elderly people. Network television has all but turned its back on viewers older than 50, and the graying of America is not accurately reflected in prime-time television (Kogan, 1992). Kogan's article concludes by posing the question of whether it is television's job to serve viewers or advertisers. "I don't think you want to hear the answer to that question," one ABC executive responded.

TELEVISION NEWS AND ELDERLY PEOPLE

Local television is rapidly becoming a prime source of news (Peale & Harmon, 1991). The people responsible for the news decisions that transform everyday events into the sights and sounds of the evening newscast also are held responsible for building the public agenda of issues and events. If newspapers reflect society's concerns (Wass, Almerico, Campbell, & Tatum, 1984), then the same can be said for television news. Fisher (1977) says society's concerns do not include elderly people or the issue of aging.

In a study of television's effect on adults, Gans (1968) found that one-third of the respondents felt that television helped them understand their personal problems and make decisions, particularly when they could identify the situation being presented. Gans' findings suggested that examining television programming to identify messages about human life in general is appropriate, and can be applied to specific categories of individuals, such as older adults.

A number of studies have focused on gratifications sought and obtained from television news (Davis & Edwards, 1975; Rubin & Rubin, 1981; Wenner, 1984). These studies indicate that for some the content of newscasts provides information of value in personal and social situations. For others the process of viewing news may be an end in itself, because of its entertainment values and its ability to reduce feelings of social isolation. The television is readily accessible, provides a link to the outside world, allows the elderly to structure time periods of their day, and provides companionship.

Five gratifications have been identified (Palmgreen, Wenner, & Rayburn, 1980) which may provide insight into the television news viewing behaviors of the elderly. The five gratifications are:
1) general information seeking, 2) decisional utility,
3) entertainment, 4) interpersonal unity, and 5) para-social interaction.

Research by Levine (1986) found that major market local television newscasts include very substantial doses of helplessness. Members of the general public are most often presented as helpless, and by implication, so are most viewers.

There are several reasons that local news may be the basis for social reality perceptions by the elderly, beyond the fact that it is heavily watched and a part of regular daily activities. Local news is dramatic and often watched for entertainment reasons (Dominick, Wurtzel,

& Lometti, 1975; Bogart, 1980; Rubin, Perse, & Powell, 1985), and local news is perceived as realistic by much of its audience (Rubin, Perse, & Powell, 1985). On an average evening a half-hour local newscast will have a slightly larger audience than a network newscast (Schonfeld, 1983; *Broadcasting*, March 30, 1987, pp. 163-164). Increased viewing of local television news does not mean an increase in the perception of personal safety (Perse, 1990), but it may influence an older viewer's thinking toward an issue of direct importance to them, for example Social Security (Iyengar & Kinder, 1987).

Content analyses of network and local television newscasts show an absence of stories relating to social issues which might be of importance to elderly people (Stempel, 1988). Adams (1978) conducted an analysis of ten Pennsylvania television stations, and found an emphasis on local politics, not on sensational and human interest stories. Non-political community and organization activity received less than one and a half minutes of coverage, or about nine percent of total news time. Harmon found in a 1989 case study of Cincinnati that most of the stories fell into the police/fire/executive/courts categories. Pollack (1989) argued that the media have done an incomplete job of educating themselves about social policy questions that affect the elderly. He says too many editors see the problems of elderly people as too boring or depressing for regular coverage.

It may be that the problems facing elderly people are seen as boring or depressing because those problems are not viewed through the eyes of older Americans. In Gerbner's (1993) analysis of women and minorities on television, he found minority groups other than women featured in only three percent of the network news stories analyzed. The newsmakers themselves were less likely to be older adults. Twelve percent of the male newsmakers were over 60 years of age, six percent of the women were over 60, and one percent or less of other minorities were over 60.

Smith (1988) found in his research that as satellite technology makes more out-of-town stories available to local television, and as network news budgets continue to shrink, dependency on local television news may grow. He called for future research on the degree to which television news meets audience psychological and social needs as opposed to audience desires for diversion.

Of all the media, television offers the most frequent view of older people (Tebbel, 1975). Consequently, television is in a better position to eliminate misunderstandings. That has not been the case. In a Cable News Network special focusing attention on people 50 years of age and older (1993), gerontologist Ken Dychtwald noted that the media should be leading the charge in creating a more contemporary image of aging: "But the media, whether it's the movies or TV, are probably about ten years behind." Sociologist Myrna Lewis said the media is having an identity crisis: "They are faced with the demographics of their readership and their viewership, all of which are moving toward old age in enormous numbers. But, they cannot, personally, face this issue. So, I think they are denying the fact that the demographics are there and they cannot quite accept them, yet."

Previous studies concerning television's portrayal of elderly people have not adequately addressed TV news. The attitudes of television general managers and news directors toward elderly people, and the issues of importance to the elderly, must be understood.

III

Methodology

The objective of the present study was to use the Kogan Attitudes Toward Old People scale (1961) in gathering data from television general managers and news directors. The data was used to describe their attitudes toward elderly people. These responses, and the resulting index, may provide information on whether or not older adults are considered a crucial part of the television news viewing audience.

Shaw and Wright (1967) found the Kogan Attitudes Toward Old People scale (OP) to be carefully developed and used with some success in a number of studies. However, they point out that the scale may have some response bias. Shaw and Wright suggest that the matched positive and negative items should compensate for this to some extent. Another potential problem with the Kogan scale is the wording of the statements. The language used in the Kogan scale reflects how society viewed elderly people thirty-plus years ago. For comparison purposes the wording has been left intact.

The Kogan scale, despite its deficiencies, is the best available one for doing large-scale survey research. A symposium at the 1993 meeting of the Gerontological Society in New Orleans featured current research using the scale. Those papers included research into conversational management (Ryan, Boich, & Wiemann, 1993), studies of medical students (Merrill, Laux, Lorimor, Thornby, & Vallbona, 1993), and mental health professionals (Rose, Coen, & Gatz, 1993). Other research investigated the effect of expectations on helping behavior of partners toward the elderly (Reicher & Baltes, 1993), and examined the attitude, age and typicality judgments of stereotypes of the elderly (Hummert, Garstka, Bonnesen, & Strahm, 1993).

The OP scale has been used in studies of attitudes toward the aged held by college students (Kogan, 1961; Thorson, 1975; Auerback & Levenson, 1977; Thorson & Perkins, 1981; Murphy-Russell, Die, & Walker, 1986; Kremer, 1988; Powell, Thorson, Kara, & Uhl, 1990), nursing home nurses (Bagshaw & Adams, 1986; Chandler, Rachel, & Kazelskis, 1986), and practicing physicians (Hellbusch, 1994), among others. It has been shown to have acceptable levels of validity and reliability.

The attitudes of the television general managers and news directors toward elderly people will be compared with the results from previous studies that used the Kogan scale.

DEFINITION OF TERMS

Any research dealing with elderly people is not without a methodological problem: defining what is meant by "elderly." For purposes of this study the socially-defined chronological age of 65 will be used (U.S. Senate, 1987).

"Attitudes" will be defined as positive or negative positions a person takes toward experiences, physical objects, people, and/or ideas (Atchley, 1991). Atchley wrote that attitudes contain elements of both emotional liking or disliking, and positive or negative cognitive evaluation. Attitudes may develop out of personal experiences, but often they are extensions of beliefs and values.

RESEARCH QUESTIONS

The limitations of current research on television general managers' and news directors' attitudes toward elderly people, and issues of importance to them, led to the following research questions:

1. What are the attitudes of television general managers and news directors toward elderly people? What are their perceptions about issues of importance to elderly people?

2. Do these two groups differ in their attitudes toward elderly people?

3. Are there educational, age, or gender factors involved in any similarity or differences between the two groups?

DESCRIPTION OF THE INSTRUMENT

The Kogan Attitudes Toward Old People scale (OP) consists of 17 statements, each of which is phrased positively and then negatively. This means that half of the statement scores were reversed during the scoring process. Responses to the statements were scored using a Likert (agree/disagree) format numbered 1,2,3,5,6,7, from strongly disagree (1) to strongly agree (7). Blank statements were assigned a score of 4. Using this method, the lower a respondent's total or mean score, the more positive were that person's attitudes toward elderly people. The television managers also responded to a series of statements on their views about news coverage. Once again the scoring method detailed above was used. Additionally, ten hypothetical story topics that affect younger and older people were used as a measure of interest using the Kogan scoring method. Finally, respondents answered a number of demographic questions, and were given the opportunity to identify other issues or survey problems through an open-ended question.

POPULATION AND THE SAMPLING

General managers and news directors at commercial television stations across the United States were selected in a probability sample. Market size was utilized in determining a stratified random sample (Babbie, 1992) using the 1993 *Broadcasting & Cable Market Place*. This yearbook is more comprehensive than other directories in that it gives lists by station rather than by membership of individuals; it is commonly used in mass media research (Wimmer & Dominick, 1994).

Individual general managers and news directors were randomly selected to represent each of the 209 television markets, rather than a sample of the total television general manager and news director population. The sample represents roughly equal numbers of general managers and news directors for comparative purposes.

DATA COLLECTION PROCEDURES

A total of 418 management-level employees were identified for the survey mailing list. Each person on the mailing list received a pre-notification letter explaining the purpose of the survey and informing them that they would receive a survey within 72 hours (Wimmer & Dominick, 1994). The survey was to be self-administered.

The Total Design Method for mail surveys was used (Dillman, 1979). Personalized cover-letters, surveys (Appendix) and business reply envelopes were sent. The first wave of surveys were mailed in October 1993. A reminder postcard was sent 72 hours later, and a second mailing of the survey to non-respondents followed about 72 hours after the postcard.

ANALYSIS OF THE DATA

SPSSx, version 4.1, software mounted on a VAX, Deck 5400 computer was used to process the data obtained from the sample. Measures of central tendency were obtained including means and standard deviations for the total sample, and sub-samples.

General managers and news directors were compared. Index scores for the occupation groups were computed. T-tests were executed for independent samples based on occupational groups, as well as a breakdown of the statements. The index scores for general managers and news directors were compared with previous studies that utilized the OP scale. Comparisons were done using baseline data.

DIRECTIONAL HYPOTHESES

1. Television general managers will be more positive than news directors toward older people.

2. Older respondents will be more positive than younger respondents toward older people.

3. The comparison groups will be more positive than both occupational groups toward older people.

IV

Quantitative Results

Of the 418 television general managers and news directors sampled, 162 returned the survey, for a response rate of 38.8 percent. This is typical for a mail survey (Wimmer & Dominick, 1994). Within the occupational groups, 81 news directors responded to the survey, 76 general managers responded, and five of the returned surveys did not provide occupational information. Based on a total of 209 television markets, the median market size for responding news directors was 93.5, and the median market size for responding general managers was 99.

Only three of the general manager respondents were 65 or older. In the 50-plus age category, there were 34 general managers (44.7 percent) and eleven news directors (13.6 percent).

Demographic differences existed between the two occupational groups (see Table 1). The median age for general managers in the sample was 49, and the median age for news directors was 40. White males dominated both occupational groups -- 97 percent of general managers were men compared with 79 percent of news directors, and 97 percent of general managers were white compared with 91 percent of news directors.

Most general managers and news directors had attended college. Eighty-eight percent of the general managers and 83 percent of the news directors had completed college. More than a quarter of the responding general managers and news directors had taken graduate courses; 15 percent of the general managers and ten

Table 1
Demographic Description of Television General Managers and News Directors

Variables	(N=76) GMs	(N=81) NDs	(N=162) Total
Median Age	49	40	45
Gender			
Male	97.4%	79.0%	87.9%
Female	2.6%	21.0%	12.1%
Race			
White	97.3%	91.4%	94.2%
African American	1.4%	2.5%	1.9%
Native American	1.4%	3.7%	2.6%
Hispanic American	0.0%	2.5%	1.3%
Educational Level Attended/Completed			
High School	0.0%	2.5%	1.3%
Some College	12.2%	14.8%	13.5%
Completed College	51.4%	56.8%	54.2%
Some Graduate College courses	21.6%	16.0%	18.7%
Advanced Degree	14.9%	9.9%	12.3%
College Major			
Communication*	47.2%	69.2%	58.7%
Business	23.6%	6.4%	14.7%
Liberal Arts	18.1%	15.4%	16.7%
Other	11.1%	9.0%	10.0%

Table 1 (continued)
Demographic Description of Television
General Managers
and News Directors

Variables	(N=76) GMs	(N=81) NDs	(N=162) Total
Marital Status			
Never Married	4.1%	10.0%	7.0%
Married	89.2%	77.5%	83.4%
Divorced/Widowed	6.7%	12.5%	9.6%
Median Number of Children	2	2	2
Household Income			
$10-20,000	0.0%	1.3%	0.7%
$20-35,000	1.4%	15.8%	8.7%
$35-50,000	1.4%	27.6%	14.7%
Over $50,000	97.2%	55.3%	76.0%
Individual Income			
$10-20,000	0.0%	5.3%	2.7%
$20-35,000	1.4%	22.7%	12.1%
$35-50,000	2.8%	32.0%	17.4%
Over $50,000	95.8%	40.0%	67.8%

*Communication includes Mass Communication, Journalism, Speech, and Broadcasting.

percent of the news directors held a graduate degree.

Eighty-nine percent of general managers and 77.5 percent of news directors were married. A higher percentage of news directors had either never been married or were divorced. The median number of children for both groups was two.

General managers (GMs) reported a higher household and individual income when compared with news directors (NDs). Ninety-seven percent of GMs had a household income above $50,000, and 96 percent reported an individual income above that figure. Fifty-five percent of NDs had a household income above $50,000, and 40 percent had an individual income above that figure.

KOGAN ATTITUDES TOWARD OLD PEOPLE STATEMENTS

The broadcasters who responded to this survey had an overall mean score on the Kogan Attitudes Toward Old People scale of 103.50 (see Table 2). The television general managers' mean score was 105.01, while the news directors' score was 102.07. Table 2 gives a comparison of OP scores with other groups. The lower the groups' score, the more positive the groups' attitude toward elderly people. Hellbusch (1994) noted that the practicing physicians score of 96.87 was the lowest mean score ever reported in a study.

The television general managers and news directors responded to the 34 statements that compose the Kogan Attitudes Toward Old People scale (see Table 3). The statement with the strongest overall mean was "The elderly have the same faults as anybody else" (5.97). Other statements where the overall mean was at the "slightly agree" level or higher are: "Most elderly would work as long as possible rather than be dependent;" "The

Table 2
Comparison of Kogan Attitudes Toward Old People Scores

Study	N	Score	S.D.
Hilt (1994)			
Television Managers	157	103.50	16.20
General Managers	76	105.01	16.72
News Directors	81	102.07	15.66
Kogan (1961)			
Boston University			
undergrads	168	119.01	21.94
Northeastern U.			
undergrads I	128	118.97	20.70
Northeastern U.			
undergrads II	186	114.59	22.75
Thorson (1975)			
University of Georgia			
graduates			
& undergraduates	212	108.51	21.95
Powell, Thorson, Kara, & Uhl (1990)			
Creighton U. Medical students			
Freshman	277	102.56	16.14
Seniors	232	99.95	16.79
Hellbusch (1994)			
Practicing Physicians			
in Omaha	200	96.87	15.25

Table 3
Comparison of Television General Managers and News Directors on Kogan Attitudes Toward Old People Statements

Statement(overall mean)	Group	Means*	S.D.	tvalue**
A nice residential neighborhood has a number of elderly living in it (5.25).	GMs NDs	5.12 5.37	1.38 1.09	1.28
Most elderly would work as long as possible rather than be dependent (5.85).	GMs NDs	5.82 5.88	0.74 1.02	0.43
If the elderly expect to be liked, they should eliminate their irritating faults (2.57).	GMs NDs	2.79 2.36	1.45 1.23	2.02**
It is foolish to claim that wisdom comes with old age (3.50).	GMs NDs	3.79 3.22	1.83 1.72	2.00**
It would be better if most elderly lived in residential units that also housed younger people (4.00).	GMs NDs	3.97 4.02	1.64 1.70	0.19
Most elderly seem to be quite clean in their personal appearance (5.36).	GMs NDs	5.38 5.33	0.98 1.18	-0.28
In general most elderly are alike (2.08).	GMs NDs	2.25 1.93	1.23 0.95	1.85

Table 3 (continued)
Comparison of Television General Managers and
News Directors
on Kogan Attitudes Toward Old People Statements

Statement(overall mean)	Group	Means*	S.D.	tvalue**
Most elderly make one feel ill at ease (2.00).	GMs NDs	2.08 1.93	0.93 1.01	0.98
Most elderly bore others by talking about the "good old days" (2.39).	GMs NDs	2.61 2.20	1.30 1.04	2.18**
Most elderly are cheerful, agreeable, and good humored (4.29).	GMs NDs	4.53 4.07	1.46 1.62	-1.83
Most elderly are as easy to understand as younger people (5.07).	GMs NDs	5.29 4.86	1.14 1.56	-1.94
Most elderly complain about the behavior of the younger generation (4.26).	GMs NDs	4.16 4.36	1.59 1.58	-0.79
Most elderly can adjust when the situation demands it (4.97).	GMs NDs	4.84 5.10	1.39 1.31	1.19
Most elderly need no more love and reassurance than anyone else (3.95)	GMs NDs	4.20 3.72	1.60 1.64	-1.86

Table 3 (continued)
Comparison of Television General Managers and News Directors
on Kogan Attitudes Toward Old People Statements

Statement(overall mean)	Group	Means*	S.D.	tvalue**
Most elderly spend too much time prying into the affairs of others (2.26).	GMs NDs	2.43 2.10	1.10 0.68	2.31**
Most elderly keep a clean home (5.29).	GMs NDs	5.17 5.40	1.15 1.14	1.23
The elderly have too much power in business and politics (2.79).	GMs NDs	2.78 2.80	1.23 1.31	-0.13
Most elderly would quit work as soon as pensions can support them (2.48).	GMs NDs	2.51 2.44	0.97 0.99	0.44
The elderly have the same faults as anybody else (5.97).	GMs NDs	5.99 5.96	0.64 0.87	-0.19
People grow wiser with the coming of old age (4.51).	GMs NDs	4.28 4.73	1.42 1.40	2.01**
It would be better if most elderly lived in residential units with people their own age (2.70).	GMs NDs	2.72 2.68	1.16 1.17	0.24

Table 3 (continued)
Comparison of Television General Managers and News Directors
on Kogan Attitudes Toward Old People Statements

Statement(overall mean)	Group	Means*	S.D.	tvalue**
Most elderly should be more concerned with their appearance (2.66).	GMs NDs	2.82 2.51	1.25 1.01	1.71
Most elderly are very different from one another (5.23).	GMs NDs	5.30 5.16	1.37 1.43	-0.64
Most elderly are very relaxing to be with (5.06).	GMs NDs	5.00 5.11	1.07 1.19	0.61
The elderly's accounts of their past experiences are interesting (5.47).	GMs NDs	5.38 5.56	1.01 1.04	1.07
Most elderly are irritable, grouchy, and unpleasant (2.13).	GMs NDs	2.13 2.14	0.62 0.95	-0.03
The elderly seldom complain about the behavior of younger people (3.15).	GMs NDs	3.32 2.99	1.24 1.15	-1.73
It's hard to figure out what makes the elderly tick (2.64).	GMs NDs	2.67 2.60	1.12 1.13	0.37
Most elderly are set in their ways (4.53).	GMs NDs	4.59 4.47	1.46 1.52	0.52

Table 3 (continued)
Comparison of Television General Managers and News Directors
on Kogan Attitudes Toward Old People Statements

Statement(overall mean)	Group	Means*	S.D.	tvalue**
Most elderly make excessive demands for love and reassurance (2.62).	GMs	2.76	1.19	1.68
	NDs	2.48	0.90	
Most elderly respect the privacy of others (5.26).	GMs	5.22	1.16	0.40
	NDs	5.30	1.13	
Most elderly let their homes become shabby and unattractive (2.03).	GMs	2.14	0.78	2.13**
	NDs	1.91	0.57	
The elderly have too little power in business and politics (3.36).	GMs	3.30	1.47	0.44
	NDs	3.4	1.49	
A nice residential neighborhood has few elderly living in it (2.87).	GMs	2.72	1.33	-1.18
	NDs	3.01	1.71	

*The scale is: 1=strongly disagree; 2=disagree; 3=slightly disagree; 4=no response/neutral; 5=slightly agree; 6=agree; 7=strongly agree.
**t values are pooled variance estimates. Statistically significant differences at the .05 alpha level.
The sample sizes for each group were: General Managers (N=76) and News Directors (N=81).

elderly's accounts of their past experiences are interesting;" "Most elderly seem to be quite clean in their personal appearance;" "Most elderly keep a clean home;" "Most elderly respect the privacy of others;" "A nice residential neighborhood has a number of elderly living in it;" "Most elderly are very different from one another;" "Most elderly are as easy to understand as younger people;" and, "Most elderly are very relaxing to be with." All ten of the these statements are considered positive attitudes toward the elderly.

The statement with the lowest overall mean was "Most elderly make one feel ill at ease" (2.00). Other statements where the overall mean was at the "slightly disagree" level or lower are: "Most elderly let their homes become shabby and unattractive;" "In general most elderly are alike;" "Most elderly are irritable, grouchy, and unpleasant;" "Most elderly spend too much time prying into the affairs of others;" "Most elderly bore others by talking about the 'good old days';" "Most elderly would quit work as soon as pensions can support them;" "If the elderly expect to be liked, they should eliminate their irritating faults;" "Most elderly make excessive demands for love and reassurance;" "It's hard to figure out what makes the elderly tick;" "Most elderly should be more concerned with their appearance;" "It would be better if most elderly lived in residential units with people their own age;" "The elderly have too much power in business and politics;" and, "A nice residential neighborhood has few elderly living in it." All fourteen of these statements are considered negative attitudes toward the elderly.

In six statements the overall mean was opposite the intended direction of the attitude. The statements "Most elderly complain about the behavior of the younger generation" (4.26) and "Most elderly are set in their ways" (4.53) are considered negative attitudes toward the elderly, but the overall means was on the agree side of neutral. The statements "Most elderly need no more love and reassurance than anyone else" (3.95), "The elderly have too little power in business and politics" (3.36), and "The elderly seldom complain about the behavior of younger people" (3.15) are considered positive attitudes toward the elderly, but the overall means were on the disagree side of neutral. The sixth statement, "It would be better if most elderly lived in residential units that also housed younger people" (4.00) is also considered a positive attitude toward the elderly, but the overall mean placed it at the neutral position.

In general, contrary to the hypothesis, news directors were more positive in their attitudes toward the elderly than general managers. There were statistically significant differences between the general managers and news directors on six statements. Those statements were: "If the elderly expect to be liked, they should eliminate their irritating faults;" "It is foolish to claim that wisdom comes with old age;" "Most elderly bore others by talking about the 'good old days';" "Most elderly spend too much time prying into the affairs of others;" "People grow wiser with the coming of old age;" and, "Most elderly let their homes become shabby and unattractive." In each case, news directors were more positive toward the elderly than general managers, but there was no significant difference in their overall scale scores.

KOGAN ATTITUDES TOWARD OLD PEOPLE SCALE INDEX

The overall mean for television general managers and news directors on the Kogan Attitudes Toward Old People Scale Index was 3.06 (see Table 4). The mean for the general managers

Table 4
Kogan Attitudes Toward Old People Scale Index*

	Mean	S.D.	Minimum	Maximum	Median
Overall (N=162)	3.06	0.49	2.06	4.35	2.96
General Managers (N=76)	3.09	0.49	2.06	4.35	3.02
News Directors (N=81)	3.00	0.46	2.06	4.18	2.97
Male (N=138)	3.06	0.49	2.06	4.35	2.99
Female (N=19)	2.96	0.36	2.38	3.77	2.97
Younger (N=76)**	3.00	0.45	2.06	4.18	2.96
Older (N=77)	3.05	0.45	2.09	4.24	2.97

*As indicated earlier, 17 of the 34 items in the Kogan Scale were recoded with reverse scoring, and the 34 statements were summed to create a single index score. The lower the total score, the more positive the respondent was toward elderly people. The index yielded acceptable levels of internal consistency (Chronback's alpha = .81) for the measure (Wimmer & Dominick, 1994, p. 57).

**The Younger and Older groups were defined by the median age of the responding broadcast managers. Younger respondents were those born between the years 1949 and 1969. Older respondents were those born between the years 1922 and 1948.

Table 5
Correlation Matrix of Television General Manager and News Director Responses to Kogan Attitudes Toward Old People Scale Index and Demographics

Variable	Index	Age	Education	Race	Individual Income
Index	-----				
Age	-.03	-----			
Education	-.05	-.17*	-----		
Race	.21	-.09	.07	----	
Individual Income	-.01	-.50*	.25*	-.02	----

*Pearson correlation coefficients were significant in a 2-tailed test at the .05 level.

was 3.09, and the mean for the news directors was 3.00. The mean for the male respondents was 3.06, and the mean for the nineteen female respondents was 2.96. The respondents were separated into two age groups by using the median age. The mean for the younger group (those born between 1949 and 1969) was 3.00, and the mean for the older group (those born between 1922 and 1948) was 3.05. As was stated earlier, the lower the score, the more positive the respondent's attitude was toward elderly people.

Responses of the broadcast managers on the Kogan Attitudes Toward Old People Scale Index were correlated with demographic questions (see Table 5). The strongest positive correlation was between education and individual income (.25). The strongest negative correlations were between age and individual income (-.50), and age and education (-.17). Those three correlations were statistically significant at the .05 level. However, there were no statistically significant relationships between the OP index and the demographic variables.

VIEWS ABOUT NEWS COVERAGE

The television general managers and news directors responded to ten statements concerning their views about news coverage (see Table 6). The statement with the strongest overall mean was "Exciting video helps a story" (6.01). Other statements where the overall mean was on the "slightly agree" side of neutral are: "News stories about the elderly are becoming increasingly important" (5.79); "My viewers are concerned with issues critical to older Americans" (5.57); and, "A slow-moving news story turns off viewers" (5.25).

Table 6
Comparison of Television General Managers and News Directors
on Views about News Coverage

Statement (overall mean)	Group	Means*	S.D.	t value**
Issues about or of concern to older people are hard to explain on TV (2.31).	GMs NDs	2.38 2.25	1.51 1.10	0.64
Exciting video helps a story (6.01).	GMs NDs	5.95 6.06	1.11 1.20	-0.62
A slow-moving news story turns off viewers (5.25).	GMs NDs	5.28 5.22	1.53 1.37	0.23
Stories that take a long time to unfold are not good TV (4.05).	GMs NDs	4.42 3.70	1.63 1.72	2.68**
My viewers are concerned with issues critical to older Americans (5.57).	GMs NDs	5.38 5.75	1.35 1.14	-1.87
My viewers are more likely to watch an older anchorman (4.16).	GMs NDs	3.88 4.42	1.47 1.40	-2.35**

Table 6 (continued)
**Comparison of Television General Managers and
News Directors
on Views about News Coverage**

Statement (overall mean)	Group	Means*	S.D.	t value**
My viewers are more likely to watch an older anchorwoman (3.56).	GMs NDs	3.30 3.80	1.40 1.40	-2.23**
News consultants favor a youthful look to a newscast (4.53).	GMs NDs	4.43 4.62	1.67 1.63	-0.69
News stories about the elderly are becoming increasingly important (5.79).	GMs NDs	5.66 5.91	0.99 1.06	-1.56
Newsrooms today are more likely to target older demographics (3.87).	GMs NDs	3.50 4.21	1.46 1.66	-2.84**

*The scale is: 1=strongly disagree; 2=disagree; 3=slightly disagree; 4=no response/neutral; 5=slightly agree; 6=agree; 7=strongly agree.
**t values are pooled variance estimates. Statistically significant differences at the .05 alpha level.
The sample sizes for each group were: General Managers (N=76) and News Directors (N=81).

Table 7
Comparison of Television General Managers
and News Directors
on the Importance of Certain News Stories

Statement (overall mean)	Group	Means*	S.D.	t value**
Advancement in cataract surgery (5.32).	GMs	5.24	1.28	-0.87
	NDs	5.41	1.17	
Doctor-assisted suicides (4.80).	GMs	4.43	1.65	-2.78**
	NDs	5.15	1.57	
Proposed Social Security cuts (6.10).	GMs	5.99	1.01	-1.48
	NDs	6.20	0.77	
Funding of local public education (5.78).	GMs	5.70	0.97	-0.98
	NDs	5.86	1.16	
Nursing home abuses (5.97).	GMs	5.83	1.04	-1.87
	NDs	6.10	0.75	

Table 7 (continued)
Comparison of Television General Managers and News Directors
on the Importance of Certain News Stories

Statement (overall mean)	Group	Means*	S.D.	t value**
Local property tax squabble (5.61).	GMs	5.70	1.08	1.03
	NDs	5.52	1.09	
City-enforced curfews for teens (5.36).	GMs	5.25	1.27	-1.08
	NDs	5.47	1.29	
Lower mortgage rates (5.64).	GMs	5.49	1.18	-1.71
	NDs	5.79	1.03	
Low interest rates on investments (5.33).	GMs	5.28	1.33	-0.51
	NDs	5.38	1.27	
Age discrimination lawsuits (5.39).	GMs	5.21	1.25	-1.93
	NDs	5.57	1.07	

*The scale is: 1=strongly disagree; 2=disagree; 3=slightly disagree; 4=no response/neutral; 5=slightly agree; 6=agree; 7=strongly agree.

**t values are pooled variance estimates. Statistically significant difference at the .05 alpha level.

The sample sizes for each group were: General Managers (N=76) and News Directors (N=81).

The statement with the lowest overall mean was "Issues about or of concern to older people are hard to explain on TV" (2.31). Other statements where the overall mean was on the "slightly disagree" side of neutral are: "My viewers are more likely to watch an older anchorwoman" (3.56); and, "Newsrooms today are more likely to target older demographics" (3.87). While the overall mean for the statement concerning an older anchorwoman fell on the "disagree" side of neutral, a parallel statement concerning an older anchorman (My viewers are more likely to watch an older anchorman) fell on the "agree" side of neutral (4.16).

There was a significant statistical difference between the two groups on four statements: "Stories that take a long time to unfold are not good TV"; "My viewers are more likely to watch an older anchorman"; "My viewers are more likely to watch an older anchorwoman"; and, "Newsrooms today are more likely to target older demographics." In each case the news directors' mean response leans toward a more positive view of the elderly. For example, general managers tended to disagree and news directors tended to agree that newsrooms are more likely to target older demographics.

IMPORTANCE OF CERTAIN NEWS STORIES

The television general managers and news directors responded to ten statements concerning their views on the importance of certain news stories (see Table 7). The news story with the strongest overall mean was "Proposed Social Security cuts" (6.10). All of the news stories fell on the "agree" side of neutral. The story with the lowest overall mean was "Doctor-assisted suicides" (4.80).

Table 8
Correlation Matrix of Television General Manager and News Director Responses to Kogan Attitudes Toward Old People Scale Index, Views about News Coverage, and the Importance of Certain News Stories

Statement (Views about News Coverage)	Kogan Index
Issues about or of concern to older people are hard to explain on TV.	.23*
Exciting video helps a story.	.14
A slow-moving news story turns off viewers.	.09
Stories that take a long time to unfold are not good TV.	.13
My viewers are concerned with issues critical to older Americans.	-.05

Table 8 (continued)
Correlation Matrix of Television General Manager and News Director Responses to Kogan Attitudes Toward Old People Scale Index, Views about News Coverage, and the Importance of Certain News Stories

Statement (Views about News Coverage)	Kogan Index
My viewers are more likely to watch an older anchorman.	-.05
My viewers are more likely to watch an older anchorwoman.	-.15
News consultants favor a youthful look to a newscast.	.10
News stories about the elderly are becoming increasingly important.	-.26*
Newsrooms today are more likely to target older demographics.	-.13

*Pearson correlation coefficients were significant in a 2-tailed test at the .05 level (N=162).

Table 8 (continued)
Correlation Matrix of Television General Manager and News Director Responses to Kogan Attitudes Toward Old People Scale Index, Views about News Coverage, and the Importance of Certain News Stories

Statement (Importance of Certain News)	Kogan Index
Advancement in cataract surgery.	-.16*
Doctor-assisted suicides.	-.03
Proposed Social Security cuts.	-.06
Funding of local public education.	-.10
Nursing home abuses.	-.20*
Local property tax squabble.	.01
City-enforced curfews for teens.	-.08
Lower mortgage rates.	-.22*
Low interest rates on investments.	-.12
Age discrimination lawsuits.	-.22*

*Pearson correlation coefficients were significant in a 2-tailed test at the .05 level (N=162).

On only one story was there a significant statistical difference between general managers and news directors: "Doctor-assisted suicides." In addition, except for the story "Local property tax squabble," news directors leaned more toward agreeing with the importance of each story than did general managers.

CORRELATION OF INDEX WITH VIEWS ABOUT NEWS COVERAGE AND IMPORTANCE OF CERTAIN NEWS STORIES

Responses of the broadcast managers on the Kogan Attitudes Toward Old People Scale Index were correlated with statements concerning their views about news coverage, and the importance of certain news stories (see Table 8). Out of ten items about their news coverage, two statements had statistically significant relationships with the Kogan Index: "Issues about or of concern to older people are hard to explain on TV" (r=.23); and, "News stories about the elderly are becoming increasingly important" (r=-.26). The negative correlation on this statement reflects a positive relationship, i.e, the broadcast managers with a more positive attitude toward elderly people were more likely to agree with this statement. There was a negative relationship between the two statistically significant statements (r=.-20).

Four news stories were statistically significant with the Kogan Index, and all four had negative correlations. The four news stories were: lower mortgage rates (r=-.22); age discrimination lawsuits (r=-.22); nursing home abuses (r=-.20); and, advancement in cataract surgery (r=-.16). All but one of the news stories were negative correlations with the Kogan Index.

Once again, the more negative the correlation between the OP score and any variable, the more positive the attitude.

RESPONDENTS' AGE AS A FACTOR

The respondents were divided into two groups based on their age. Those general managers and news directors born in 1949 or after were classified as younger respondents (44-years-old and younger), and those born in 1948 or before were classified as older respondents (45-years-old and older). In the 34 items that compose the Kogan Attitudes Toward Old People scale, there were statistically significant differences between the younger and older respondents on three statements (see Table 9). The three statements were: "Most elderly bore others by talking about the 'good old days';" "It is foolish to claim that wisdom comes with old age;" and, "If the elderly expect to be liked, they should eliminate their irritating faults." In each case, the more positive attitude toward the elderly is held by the younger respondents.

The general managers and news directors were divided by age into the two groups to examine their responses to ten statements concerning their views about news coverage (see Table 10). There was a statistically significant difference between the two groups on one statement: "Stories that take a long time to unfold are not good TV." The younger respondents lean more to the disagree side of neutral on that statement.

Finally, the general managers and news directors were divided by age into the two groups to look at their responses to ten statements concerning their views on the importance of certain news stories (see Table 11). On only one story was there a significant statistical difference between the two groups: "Local property tax squabble." Older respondents leaned toward agreeing

Table 9
Comparison of Younger and Older Respondents
on Kogan Attitudes Toward Old People Statements

Statement (overall mean)	Group	Means*	S.D.	t value**
A nice residential neighborhood has a number of elderly living in it (5.25).	Y	5.22	1.24	0.72
	O	5.36	1.16	
Most elderly would work as long as possible rather than be dependent (5.85).	Y	5.80	0.99	0.84
	O	5.92	0.74	
If the elderly expect to be liked, they should eliminate their irritating faults (2.57).	Y	2.28	1.16	-2.38**
	O	2.78	1.44	
It is foolish to claim that wisdom comes with old age (3.50).	Y	3.13	1.69	-2.48**
	O	3.84	1.86	
It would be better if most elderly lived in residential units that also housed younger people (4.00).	Y	3.87	1.62	0.96
	O	4.13	1.74	
Most elderly seem to be quite clean in their personal appearance (5.36).	Y	5.33	1.12	0.72
	O	5.45	1.02	
In general most elderly are alike (2.08).	Y	1.91	0.80	-1.60
	O	2.18	1.26	

Table 9 (continued)
Comparison of Younger and Older Respondents
on Kogan Attitudes Toward Old People Statements

Statement (overall mean)	Group	Means*	S.D.	t value**
Most elderly make one feel ill at ease (2.00).	Y	1.99	0.97	0.17
	O	1.96	0.94	
Most elderly bore others by talking about the "good old days" (2.39).	Y	2.13	1.02	-2.54**
	O	2.61	1.29	
Most elderly are cheerful, agreeable, and good humored (4.29).	Y	4.18	1.57	0.76
	O	4.38	1.57	
Most elderly are as easy to understand as younger people (5.07).	Y	5.01	1.46	0.63
	O	5.16	1.34	
Most elderly complain about the behavior of the younger generation (4.26).	Y	4.12	1.58	-1.00
	O	4.38	1.61	
Most elderly can adjust when the situation demands it (4.97).	Y	4.88	1.40	1.02
	O	5.10	1.29	
Most elderly need no more love and reassurance than anyone else (3.95).	Y	3.93	1.65	0.10
	O	3.96	1.66	

Table 9 (continued)
Comparison of Younger and Older Respondents
on Kogan Attitudes Toward Old People Statements

Statement (overall mean)	Group	Means*	S.D.	t value**
Most elderly spend too much time prying into the affairs of others (2.26).	Y O	2.16 2.29	0.83 0.93	-0.89
Most elderly keep a clean home (5.29).	Y O	5.42 5.18	1.01 1.26	-1.29
The elderly have too much power in business and politics (2.79).	Y O	2.88 2.68	1.34 1.21	1.00
Most elderly would quit work as soon as pensions can support them (2.48).	Y O	2.46 2.43	0.90 1.01	0.21
The elderly have the same faults as anybody else (5.97).	Y O	6.04 5.96	0.70 0.79	-0.65
People grow wiser with the coming of old age (4.51).	Y O	4.63 4.38	1.44 1.42	-1.10
It would be better if most elderly lived in residential units with people their own age (2.70).	Y O	2.75 2.58	1.19 1.08	0.90

Table 9 (continued)
Comparison of Younger and Older Respondents
on Kogan Attitudes Toward Old People Statements

Statement (overall mean)	Group	Means*	S.D.	t value**
Most elderly should be more concerned with their appearance (2.66).	Y	2.53	1.01	-1.05
	O	2.71	1.20	
Most elderly are very different from one another (5.23).	Y	5.33	1.30	-0.77
	O	5.16	1.49	
Most elderly are very relaxing to be with (5.06).	Y	5.11	1.16	-0.43
	O	5.03	1.12	
The elderly's accounts of their past experiences is interesting (5.47).	Y	5.59	0.96	-1.23
	O	5.39	1.08	
Most elderly are irritable, grouchy, and unpleasant (2.13).	Y	2.13	0.89	0.22
	O	2.10	0.66	
The elderly seldom complain about the behavior of younger people (3.15).	Y	3.16	1.12	-0.14
	O	3.13	1.29	
It's hard to figure out what makes the elderly tick (2.64).	Y	2.67	1.12	0.62
	O	2.56	1.13	
Most elderly are set in their ways (4.53).	Y	4.59	1.43	0.46
	O	4.48	1.57	

Table 9 (continued)
Comparison of Younger and Older Respondents
on Kogan Attitudes Toward Old People Statements

Statement (overall mean)	Group	Means*	S.D.	t value**
Most elderly make excessive demands for love and reassurance (2.62).	Y	2.49	0.87	-1.34
	O	2.71	1.20	
Most elderly respect the privacy of others (5.26).	Y	5.43	1.01	-1.60
	O	5.14	1.23	
Most elderly let their homes become shabby and unattractive (2.03).	Y	1.93	0.55	-1.11
	O	2.05	0.74	
The elderly have too little power in business and politics (3.36).	Y	3.38	1.44	-0.23
	O	3.32	1.55	
A nice residential neighborhood has few elderly living in it (2.87).	Y	2.96	1.69	0.88
	O	2.74	1.39	
Kogan Attitudes Toward Old People Index	Y	3.00	0.45	-0.78
	O	3.05	0.45	

*The scale is: 1=strongly disagree; 2=disagree; 3=slightly disagree; 4=no response/neutral; 5=slightly agree; 6=agree; 7=strongly agree.
**t values are pooled variance estimates. Statistically significant differences at the .05 alpha level.
The sample sizes for each group were: Younger Respondents (N=76) and Older Respondents (N=77).

Table 10
Comparison of Younger and Older Respondents
on Views about News Coverage

Statement (overall mean)	Group	Means*	S.D.	t value**
Issues about or of concern to older people are hard to explain on TV (2.31).	Y	2.32	1.20	-0.04
	O	2.32	1.44	
Exciting video helps a story (6.01).	Y	6.07	1.10	0.63
	O	5.95	1.22	
A slow-moving news story turns off viewers (5.25).	Y	5.21	1.40	-0.50
	O	5.32	1.45	
Stories that take a long time to unfold are not good TV (4.05).	Y	3.57	1.64	-3.66**
	O	4.53	1.63	
My viewers are concerned with issues critical to older Americans (5.57).	Y	5.54	1.39	-0.41
	O	5.62	1.11	
My viewers are more likely to watch an older anchorman (4.16).	Y	4.05	1.45	-1.10
	O	4.31	1.46	
My viewers are more likely to watch an older anchorwoman (3.56).	Y	3.46	1.40	-0.93
	O	3.68	1.45	

Table 10 (continued)
Comparison of Younger and Older Respondents
on Views about News Coverage

Statement (overall mean)	Group	Means*	S.D.	t value**
News consultants favor a youthful look to a newscast (4.53).	Y O	4.47 4.60	1.67 1.62	-0.46
News stories about the elderly are becoming increasingly important (5.79).	Y O	5.64 5.95	1.24 0.76	-1.83
Newsrooms today are more likely to target older demographics (3.87).	Y O	4.07 3.73	1.61 1.60	1.31

*The scale is: 1=strongly disagree; 2=disagree; 3=slightly disagree; 4=no response/neutral; 5=slightly agree; 6=agree; 7=strongly agree.
**t values are pooled variance estimates. Statistically significant differences at the .05 alpha level.
The sample sizes for each group were: Younger Respondents (N=76) and Older Respondents (N=77).

Table 11
Comparison of Younger and Older Respondents
on the Importance of Certain News Stories

Statement (overall mean)	Group	Means*	S.D.	t value**
Advancement in cataract	Y	5.21	1.36	-1.37
surgery (5.32).	O	5.48	1.06	
Doctor-assisted	Y	5.03	1.66	1.76
suicides (4.80).	O	4.56	1.63	
Proposed Social Security	Y	5.99	0.96	-1.82
cuts (6.10).	O	6.25	0.80	
Funding of local public	Y	5.92	1.08	1.66
education (5.78).	O	5.64	1.04	
Nursing home abuses (5.97).	Y	6.05	0.82	0.84
	O	5.94	0.92	

Table 11 (continued)
Comparison of Younger and Older Respondents
on the Importance of Certain News Stories

Statement (overall mean)	Group	Means*	S.D.	t value**
Local property tax	Y	5.36	1.19	-2.92**
squabble (5.61).	O	5.86	0.93	
City-enforced curfews for	Y	5.50	1.30	1.17
teens (5.36).	O	5.26	1.24	
Lower mortgage rates (5.64).	Y	5.70	1.05	0.42
	O	5.62	1.15	
Low interest rates on	Y	5.14	1.30	-1.88
investments (5.33).	O	5.53	1.25	
Age discrimination	Y	5.30	1.29	-1.23
lawsuits (5.39).	O	5.53	1.02	

*The scale is: 1=strongly disagree; 2=disagree; 3=slightly disagree; 4=no response/neutral; 5=slightly agree; 6=agree; 7=strongly agree.
**t values are pooled variance estimates. Statistically significant difference at the .05 alpha level.
The sample sizes for each group were: Younger Respondents (N=76) and Older Respondents (N=77).

with the importance of this story more than younger respondents.

DISCUSSION OF DATA

It has been well-documented that elderly people are major consumers of television, and in particular, television news. It has also been well-documented that the older adult population is large and continuing to grow in numbers. The present study set out to discover the television general managers' and news directors' attitudes toward elderly people, whether the managers consider elderly people an important part of the television news viewing audience, and whether the managers' attitudes toward the elderly impacted their view of news coverage.

RESEARCH QUESTIONS

This study posed three research questions:

1. What are the attitudes of television general managers and news directors toward elderly people? What are their perceptions about issues of importance to elderly people?

The overall score by the broadcast managers on the Kogan Attitudes Toward Old People scale was 103.50. Another way of describing the attitudes of broadcast managers toward the elderly is comparing their score with other groups that have answered the Kogan scale. For example, the television general managers and news directors responding to this survey had less negative attitudes toward the elderly than undergraduate students at Boston University and Northeastern University (Kogan, 1961), and graduates and undergraduates at the University of Georgia (Thorson, 1975). The broadcast managers had less positive attitudes toward the elderly than Creighton University medical students (Powell, Thorson, Kara, & Uhl, 1990) and practicing physicians in Omaha (Hellbusch, 1994). Kogan's (1961) three groups were students in an introductory psychology class. Thorson (1975), by comparing undergraduate student and graduate student responses, demonstrated that age and years of education have an influence on a person's attitude toward old people.

In comparing the respondents in the present study with other groups who have taken the Kogan Attitudes Toward Old People scale, the broadcasters' score was more positive than anticipated. This may have been a function of their age and professional status.

The television managers rated nearly all of the issues of importance to elderly people as important. In Table 8 of Chapter Four, the negative correlations indicate that the respondents with a positive attitude toward the elderly (lower OP score) would agree with the importance of these issues. Only one issue did not have such a correlation (local property tax squabble), and four of the ten news issues had significant negative correlations.

2. Do these two groups differ in their attitudes toward elderly people?

As noted in Table 2 of Chapter Four, between the general managers and news directors, NDs were more positive in their OP score than GMs.

Within this sample, however, there was no significant difference in the Kogan score for television news directors (102.07) and general managers (105.01) (t=1.14; p<.26).

On the issue of how the managers' attitudes relate to their views about news coverage, there was strong agreement that "Exciting video helps a story" (6.01), "News stories about the elderly are becoming increasingly important" (5.79), and "My viewers are concerned with issues critical to older Americans" (5.57). Conversely, there was strong disagreement that "Issues about or of concern to older people are hard to explain on TV" (2.31), "My viewers are more likely to watch an older anchorwoman" (3.56), and "Newsrooms today are more likely to target older demographics" (3.87). What these findings suggest is that the broadcast managers perceive a viewer interest in issues of concern to elderly people, but such news coverage needs to hold viewer attention. Obviously, exciting video does just that because the managers also agreed that "A slow-moving news story turns off viewers" (5.25).

Groups interested in increasing the amount of news coverage about issues affecting older people should offer the news media story opportunities that provide exciting, fast-paced video. Stories which show the elderly "in action" will be more likely to be covered as "news."

However, there were differences between the television general managers and news directors in their views about news coverage. While GMs leaned toward agreement that "Stories that take a long time to unfold are not good TV" (4.42), NDs leaned toward disagreement (3.70). There was a significant difference between the two groups on this item (t=2.68; p<.05).

On three other statements there were significant differences between the two groups: "Newsrooms today are more like to target older demographics" (GMs=3.50, NDs=4.21; t=-2.84; p<.05); "My viewers are more likely to watch an older anchorman" (GMs=3.88, NDs=4.42; t=-2.35; p<.05); and, "My viewers are more likely to watch an older anchorwoman" (GMs=3.30, NDs=3.80; t=-2.23; p<.05). In each statement, news directors lean more toward agreement than general managers. This pattern indicates that news directors seem to be more open-minded about the coverage of elderly issues. NDs seem to welcome the coverage of these stories, as long as those stories meet the needs of action-oriented television news. Perhaps one reason why Stempel (1988) did not find many stories relating to social issues of importance to the elderly is that the news sources failed to offer broadcast newsrooms exciting video or fast-moving news stories. For example, sources wanting television coverage of an issue should not provide only a spokesperson in a meeting room, or written information. Broadcast managers want news coverage to show examples of the issue or problem, and they want people who are affected by the issue to speak about it. Certainly, it is not always possible to frame an important social issue in a form enticing to local television news. But, when this is accomplished, it is much more likely to make the newscast.

One argument often made is that news directors would be more likely to be open-minded about the coverage of elderly issues since they may view it as a freedom of the press issue. This argument continues by assuming that general managers would be more interested in the financial picture of the station, rather than a constitutional issue. However, an earlier survey of broadcast general managers and news directors by Lipschultz and Hilt (1993) found that in spite of this temptation, the two occupational groups are supportive of both positions in most cases. In their research the First Amendment views and business orientations of radio and television general managers and news directors were rarely in conflict. What this might imply for the present study is that news directors view possible stories independently -- each story must stand on its own merit.

3. Are there educational, age, or gender factors involved in any similarity or differences between the two groups?

Tables 4 and 5 of Chapter Four address this question. There was a slight difference in the mean response to statements in the Kogan Attitudes Toward Old People scale between men and women (Table 4). However, the difference was not significant, and the nineteen women who responded to this random survey would make it difficult to generalize beyond the scope of this study. There was also a slight difference in the mean response to the Kogan statements between the younger and older age groups. But once again, the difference was not significant.

Table 5 gives the correlation between the OP index and certain demographic information. Again, the differences were not significant. This differs from Thorson's findings (1975) that age and years of education influence a person's attitude toward old people. In fact, the only significant differences in the correlation occurred within the demographics. Individual income correlated at a significant level with both age and education (the higher the income, the older and/or more educated the respondent). Education and age also correlated at a significant level.

DIRECTIONAL HYPOTHESES

Previous research suggested three directional hypotheses for the broadcast managers:

1. Television general managers will be more positive than news directors toward older people.

This hypothesis cannot be accepted, based on the data in Table 2 of Chapter Four. As a group, television news directors had more positive attitudes toward the elderly than general managers, but the difference was not statistically significant.

2. Older respondents will be more positive than younger respondents toward older people.

The data gathered in this study does not support this hypothesis. Younger respondents (those born during or after 1949) actually leaned in the direction of having a more positive attitude toward elderly people than older respondents (those born before 1949). In addition, younger respondents tended to agree that "Newsrooms today are more likely to target older demographics."

General managers were older than news directors by an average of nine years. However, NDs had a more positive attitude toward the elderly than GMs, although the difference was not significant.

3. The comparison groups will be more positive than both occupational groups toward older people.

The results of this study present a mixed response for this hypothesis. While the television general managers and news directors, as individual groups and as a whole, had lower OP scores than the students in the Kogan (1961) study and the Thorson (1975) study, the scores were higher than the students in the Powell, Thorson, Kara, & Uhl (1990) study and the practicing physicians in the Hellbusch (1994) study. This hypothesis then, cannot be accepted, since the broadcast managers were more positive in their attitudes toward the elderly than expected.

V

Qualitative Comments

Respondents were given the opportunity to provide comments or additional information at several points on the survey instrument. The instrument began with a series of ten questions asking for their views about news coverage. At the bottom of the first page respondents were given space to answer the question, "Do you have comments concerning these ten statements, or any other important issues relating to your news coverage?" The responses were varied, but can be divided into several general categories: content, demographics, and advertising.

Several respondents focused on the content of television newscasts, and how it relates to the elderly. One respondent indicated that news content, not technological bells and whistles, will attract and keep an audience. Another respondent, a 36-year-old male general manager from a Top 30 market said, "Any complex issue is difficult to explain in a typical TV news format, not just issues facing older people." A 39-year-old female news director said, "It's often difficult to get people on-camera to discuss issues of concern to the elderly -- especially the elderly."

The demographics of the television news audience, and the advertising seen in those newscasts, are linked. One 53-year-old male general manager said, "News viewers tend to be 45+. Trends point to an 'older' future viewership." A 43-year-old female news director echoed that sentiment, saying "As the population ages, older issues, older anchors, etc., become more important/interesting to viewers." And a 56-year-old male general manager added, "The news audience at our station and across the country skews to 50+ which says something about the inability of news to reach 18-49. Only a fool would alienate the bulk of your news audience, but sales pushes news to attract 18-49."

However, a 51-year-old male news director disagreed, saying "News coverage often depends on market research these days, and can be translated to viewer interests, or more specifically, to interests of a station's target audience. And it generally is not older Americans, unless you consider 35-49 old."

Market research aids advertisers in deciding to buy commercial time within a newscast. Respondents to this survey said this factor impacts what is seen on television. A 72-year-old male general manager said, "As we learn more about the importance of the elderly ($ speak) there will be a lot more coverage." A 37-year-old male news director said, "Consultants are pushing older, more distinguished anchors (male). Unfortunately, they still push younger females. Our target demo is people 18-49. However, we also cater to our older viewers. We do a weekly public affairs program geared toward older viewers." A 52-year-old male general manager agreed, saying "Most newsrooms do tend to skew their coverage to attract younger demos. We are located in the oldest skewing ADI in the country, therefore our approach is different." And a 33-year-old male news director said, "In our area winter retirees are a key component of our audience, but this is a smaller market so talent tends to be young because many are beginning their careers."

Some respondents placed the blame for the lack of elderly news within television newscasts at the feet of advertisers. A 45-year-old male general manager said, "Advertisers have not recognized the population shift and importance of the 55+ demo. Advertisers drive the financial forces of the TV business, thus 55+ gets short changed in coverage." A 61-year-old male general manager said, "Older Americans are healthy, vigorous, have huge buying power, and are more concerned with news locally, nationally, and globally. They should be catered to by advertisers." A 47-year-old female news director said, "We believe seniors are becoming increasingly important to all issues. Economically more powerful." And a 42-year-old male news director said, "Sales departments prefer younger audiences to increase revenue. Most general managers come out of the sales departments. They pressure news directors to deliver younger audiences."

Two respondents seemed to summarize best the feelings of those who took the time to answer the open-ended question. A 44-year-old male news director said, "Older viewers are more likely to be regular news viewers. Younger demos are more attractive to sales. You need them both to win ratings." And a 57-year-old male general manager said, "It seems obvious that future news broadcasts may well be targeted to particular age groups, say 18-49 and 25-60, with anchors, content, and production techniques tailored to viewers of different ages."

Respondents were given the opportunity to discuss the appearance of their anchor team by answering the open-ended question "What attributes would the "ideal" TV news anchor team possess?" Those responding to the question usually listed several keys words to highlight what they look for in a television news anchor. "Knowledge of the local community" was the leading attribute mentioned, with "Credibility" a close second. Some of the other attributes mentioned, in descending order, were "Strong communication/journalism skills," "Attractiveness," and "Maturity."

Respondents were also given the opportunity to answer specific questions concerning their own stations' practice of attracting elderly viewers (see Table 12).

Finally, respondents were given the opportunity to comment on the research instrument itself, or on the issue of elderly viewers and television news, at the end of the survey. The question posed was "Do you have any other comments on topics raised in this survey?"

Most respondents used this space to address the larger issue of the elderly and television. A 39-year-old female news director said, "We've go to do more on the elderly" while admitting that "Our communities have one of the highest concentrations of retirees in the nation." A 29-year-old male news director said, "We serve a rural and aging population. We include a regular segment aired three times a week on senior issues." A 46-year-old male news director said, "As 'boomers' mature *most* media will follow them; hence, there will be more emphasis on older demos."

One 45-year-old male general manager captured the problem of attracting advertisers while serving the viewing audience by saying, "Focus on educating advertisers of the economic value of 55+. TV stations will program to advertisers' interests to gain $. If advertisers recognize 55+, news and programming will follow. Do not forget we are a bottom-line business."

Table 12
Comparison of Television General Managers
and News Directors
on local newscasts and older viewers

Statement	Group	Agree	Disagree
Our station is interested in in attracting viewers of all ages for our local newscasts.	GM ND	73(96.1%) 78(96.3%)	2(2.6%) 3(3.7%)
Older viewers are an important segment of our local news audience.	GM ND	73(96.1%) 76(93.8%)	2(2.6%) 5(6.2%)
Our local newscasts are targeted at older viewers.	GM ND	13(17.1%) 15(18.5%)	60(78.9%) 64(79.0%)

VI

Conclusion

A consistent theme in gerontological literature is that negative attitudes toward aging influence how a person cares for or perceives the elderly (Powell, Thorson, Kara, & Uhl, 1990). The present study sought to identify the broadcast managers' attitudes toward the elderly. The types of news stories or newscasts that air on a television station are influenced by the broadcast managers. Therefore, those managers' attitudes toward the elderly could influence those stories or programs.

Through correlating the Kogan Attitudes Toward Old People score with the managers' views of news coverage, it is possible to determine whether older adults are considered a crucial part of the television news viewing audience. In the present study, respondents seemed to say 'yes' -- older adults are indeed an important part of the audience. In Table 8 of Chapter Four, two statements were found to be significant when correlating the OP score with the managers' views about news coverage: "Issues about or of concern to older people are hard to explain on TV" (r=.23) and "News stories about the elderly are becoming increasingly important" (r=-.26). The positive relationship with the first statement means those respondents who had a positive attitude toward the elderly disagreed with the statement. The negative relationship with the second statement means those who had a positive attitude toward the elderly agreed with the statement.

These results indicate that the broadcast managers realize the need to please their older audience. This would support research conducted by the ABC Television Network. Wurtzel (1992) found that the number of people watching the network newscasts has declined since 1980. The changing media environment that offered viewers an array of choices -- independent stations, cable television, pay television, and VCRs -- was one reason. The fragmentation of the marketplace hurt the networks. Wurtzel found that viewers were becoming increasingly restless as a result of the increased choices. The use of the remote control device, and "surfing" or "grazing" through the available channels, had become widespread. Viewers no longer gave their undivided attention to one channel.

Wurtzel found another set of reasons for the decline in viewing. Viewers listed changing lifestyles, such as a change in their work status and increasing activities for themselves and their children, as reasons for a decline in their television viewing habits.

While Wurtzel's information applied to all television programming, he wrote that the key to both network and local stations is news viewing. He examined each age group within the population, and found that the number of people watching the newscasts within each successive generation has declined, and as each age group grows older, their viewing level changes very little. Until the mid-1960s all age groups exhibited a similar attention to news. However, since then, older adults pay much greater attention to the news while younger viewers show a decreased interest.

Wurtzel's research also found that older viewers were significantly more interested in news than other age groups, and were more likely to receive their news from television newscasts and newspapers. Younger viewers were more accepting of new news sources, such as the Cable News Network. Younger viewers considered alternatives, such as talk shows like *Oprah* or *Donahue*, and daily magazine shows like *Inside Edition* or *Hard Copy*, as valid news sources.

Wurtzel interpreted this to mean that the networks must do a better job of finding out what its news viewers want in the way of stories, and then give it to them. The problem for television general managers and news directors is determining which audience to seek, the younger audience that is attracted to the alternative news programs or the older audience that is more interested in the newscasts offered by the networks and local stations. The results in the present study would seem to indicate that the broadcast managers realize the need to please their older audience, since they agreed that "News stories about the elderly are becoming increasingly important."

Lieberman and McCray (1994) maintained that news and information needed to be relevant to all groups, if the media wanted to keep its audiences. They found that 90 percent of people at retirement age or over said keeping up with the news is extremely important.

One way to know what older viewers want would be for the television stations to employ them. Lieberman and McCray wrote that journalism has long been identified as a young person's game -- the hard work and long hours tend to discourage the family man or woman. It is not unusual to see talented journalists move into corporate or academic positions as they mature. Yet, if the news media is to develop a diverse work force to address the needs of a diverse audience, news management needs to rethink its emphasis on youth.

In the present study, only three general managers were 65 years of age or older. None of the television news directors were 65 or older. In the 50-plus category, there were 34 general managers (44.7 percent) and eleven news directors (13.6 percent). These numbers are comparable with those presented in a national survey of journalists by Weaver and Wilhoit (1992). In their survey, the number of journalists (print and broadcast) 55 to 64 years old has declined since 1971, suggesting fewer older people working in the field of journalism now than two decades ago. Since the television general manager may be comparable to the editor or publisher at a newspaper, it may be more accurate to compare the Weaver and Wilhoit results with the television news director. In that case, 22 percent of the respondents in their survey were 45 years old or older, and the median age for all of the respondents was 36. The median age for broadcast journalists, which included all types of jobs in a broadcast newsroom, was 32. In the present study, 13.6 percent of news directors were 50 or older. The median age for news directors was 40, and the median age for all of the responding broadcast managers was 46.

The median age for all of the groups surveyed, both in this study and the one by Weaver and Wilhoit, is rising. The overall median age in the present study compares with a median age of 44 found in an earlier survey of television general managers and news directors (Lipschultz & Hilt, 1992). Weaver and Wilhoit reported a median age for all journalists of 32 in 1982, compared with the median age of 36 found ten years later.

The attitudes of broadcast managers toward aging and older Americans may change as the managers grow older. At least that has been the case with the general population. In a nationwide survey of the general public, Clements (1993) found that the perception of aging improves as one grows older. Overall, 27 percent of those surveyed think of growing old as something bad. However, this figure was lower among the older responding age groups. Forty-five percent of the respondents thought life for the elderly had gotten better in the past twenty years. But, 87 percent of those polled said Americans place too much emphasis on youth.

Broadcast managers can work on changing that perception by presenting a more positive view of the aging process.

LIMITATIONS

There are advantages and disadvantages to a mailed survey. The advantages are: the ability to cover a wide geographic area, in this case the United States; the ability to provide anonymity; and, the relatively low cost.

The disadvantages are: the surveys must be self-explanatory; mail surveys are the slowest form of data collection; the researcher never knows exactly who answers the questions; replies are often received only from people who are interested in the survey, which injects bias into the results; and, the typically low return rate, which impacts the reliability and generalizability of the findings. In the present study, the response rate was 38.8 percent. According to Wimmer and Dominick (1994), this is near the high end of what is considered a typical response rate (20 to 40 percent) for mail surveys in mass media research. Singletary (1994) found return rates of 30 to 40 percent in mail surveys common for mass communication research.

One theory for the lower response rate among mass communicators is the number of surveys broadcast managers are asked to complete. Several respondents, while taking the time to complete and return the survey, took the opportunity to complain about the number of questionnaires that cross their desks. Given the response rate, it might be reasonable to assume that other broadcast managers felt the same way and simply refused to return the survey.

Sample size is another limitation to the present study. A larger sample would have allowed for more in-depth analysis of sub-groups such as women, minorities, and various age groups. For example, a larger sample would enable a breakdown of the respondents into "younger, female news directors" to compare to "older, male general managers."

There are limitations to the usefulness of the Kogan Attitudes Toward Old People scale. Respondents complained about the length of the scale (34 statements), and the transparency of the items. Some respondents wrote that the statements were stereotypes, and by answering the survey they would be verifying those stereotypes. One 36-year-old general manager seemed to summarize these comments best when he said, "I thought that the section regarding attitudes toward older people was ridiculously broad and the questions were incredibly stereotyped. I would never want to be included in a question beginning with 'most elderly.'" Further, there is a limited connection between the scale items and the more abstract social disengagement theory. Based on the social disengagement theory, the broadcast managers should have had higher OP scores, which would mean a less positive attitude toward the elderly. It is difficult to directly compare the Kogan scores in this study with previous respondents because of potential changes over the past thirty years in how society views elderly people. It is interesting to note that some of the lowest scores, and thus the more positive attitudes toward the elderly, have come when the OP scale has been administered during the 1990s. Since those lower scores were achieved using a scale developed around 1960, it may be that those respondents were able to see through the "transparent and stereotypical" statements, and selected a response that made themselves appear to have a positive attitude.

Nevertheless, the results in this study do not support the basic premise of the social disengagement theory. The attitudes of the broadcast managers toward the elderly *were* positive. Further, the broadcast managers expressed the view that "News stories about the elderly are becoming increasingly important," and that their viewers "...are concerned with issues critical to older Americans." As it becomes more and more obvious to the broadcasters that older Americans make up the bulk of their news viewing audience, we will begin to see news stories and newscasters that reflect that fact.

FUTURE RESEARCH

The Kogan Attitudes Toward Old People scale, while useful when developed more than thirty years ago, has not changed with the times. Societal views toward the elderly have modified since the early 1960s. These changes are not reflected in the scale. Before future research can be conducted, the scale should be revised. Following the suggestions made by respondents to the present study, the length of the scale should be shortened by nearly half. In addition, greater care should be taken with the wording of the items to make sure the language will not be offensive to certain members of the population. For example, the name of the scale -- the Kogan Attitudes Toward Old People scale -- may raise eyebrows itself since the term "old people" is not commonly used now to describe the elderly. Some of the statements in the scale reinforce stereotypes, such as: older adults pry into the affairs of others; they seek political and economic power; older adults are wiser merely because they are older; and, they bore others by talking about the "good old days." These statements were cited by some of the respondents as examples of why they thought the scale was biased. Future research will want to update the language used in the scale, and avoid obvious stereotypical remarks.

Future research also should focus attention on the group of newsroom employees who put a newscast together -- assignment editors and news producers. Assignment editors determine which stories will be covered by reporters and photographers, send those news crews to the story, and make sure that all of the news of the day is available for airing in the station's newscasts. Producers decide which stories run in a newscast, and the order of the stories within a newscast. While general managers and news directors set the policy for news coverage, assignment editors and producers carry out that policy on a day-to-day basis. To paraphrase Herbert Gans (1979), assignment editors and producers are the gatekeepers who decide what is news. The results of the present study suggest the need to know how assignment editors and producers would respond to the Kogan items, and their views about news coverage. Little research has been conducted on these groups. However, assignment editors and news producers are likely to be college graduates under the age of 40. While news directors in the present study were younger on average than general managers, they leaned toward having a more positive attitude toward the elderly. Both assignment editors and producers will have an average age that is younger than either of these two groups -- will that make a difference in their attitude toward older people? Both general managers and news directors agreed that "Exciting video helps a story" and "A slow-moving news story turns off viewers." How will assignment editors and producers, who must select the stories and the video, balance these views with their attitudes toward elderly people? Assignment editors and producers are the people who make those types of decisions every day.

The competition for viewers, as the ABC research notes, has gone beyond three over-the-air channels dividing the audience pie. With cable, pay television, and other sources vying for a share of the audience, local television stations feel pressure to compete. Many times that competition forces newsroom managers to sacrifice news stories that are slow-moving or those which lack interesting video in favor of those which are more visually compelling. By dividing the pie seven or eight ways rather than three or four, the economy of broadcasting also is affected. The profitability of broadcast stations in the late 1970s and early 1980s has given way to a leaner industry. There even has been discussion that not all station or network newscasts will survive. Future research in this area will go beyond determining the attitudes of broadcasters toward older people. It will help explore the future of broadcast journalism.

In light of census projections that show the elderly population increasing dramatically in the next century, and considering the importance of local television news in the lives of the elderly, the study of the attitudes of broadcasters toward older people will be increasingly relevant. Studying this group is important. As Kremer (1988) found, students with negative attitudes toward older adults showed no change when presented negative information about older people, though they did exhibit a more negative attitude about themselves. However, when presented with factual information about aging, the attitudes of the participants toward older adults and themselves improved. Studying the group that delivers information may help society understand and perceive a more accurate picture of elderly people.

Bliese (1982) may have stated it best: "We cannot blame the media for our dread of growing old. That dread has led many persons to risk life and limb in search of a 'Fountain of Youth.' We can ask the media to present old age realistically — neither ignoring it, nor debasing it, nor glorifying it. We can also ask the media to serve the needs of the older population more adequately than they are now doing. Currently most prime-time programming has been aimed at the magical eighteen to thirty-four age group, which advertisers are only now beginning to realize is rapidly shrinking in both numbers and monetary resources. As the older groups grow in numbers and monetary resources, advertisers may begin to listen to their demands and the balance may be restored. Then the media and real-life interactions may become reasonably similar in substance and form. At least one can hope" (p. 581-582).

The results of this study might have been expected. Thorson (1995) concluded by noting that the older population is the fastest growing segment of American society, well-educated, and increasingly prosperous, with the lowest poverty rate of any age group in the population. As the median age of the U.S. population grows older, it could be reasoned that broadcast managers will themselves be increasingly sensitized to what it means to be "older." As they learn more about this new market of older people, it is likely that their stereotypes about the elderly will decline.

Appendix

A SURVEY OF TELEVISION GENERAL MANAGERS AND NEWS DIRECTORS

The first section asks for your views about news coverage.

Q-1 Do you agree or disagree with the following statements? Please do not skip any items. Circle your answer for each. (1=strongly disagree, 7=strongly agree)

1 Issues about or of concern to
   older people are hard to explain
   on TV...1 2 3 5 6 7

2 Exciting video helps a story............1 2 3 5 6 7

3 A slow-moving news story
   turns off viewers................................1 2 3 5 6 7

4 Stories that take a long time to
   unfold are not good TV....................1 2 3 5 6 7

5 My viewers are concerned with
   issues critical to older Americans....1 2 3 5 6 7

6 My viewers are more likely to watch
   an older anchorman...........................1 2 3 5 6 7

7 My viewers are more likely to watch
   an older anchorwoman.....................1 2 3 5 6 7

8 News consultants favor a youthful
   look to a newscast..............................1 2 3 5 6 7

9 News stories about the elderly
   are becoming increasingly
   important..1 2 3 5 6 7

10 Newsrooms today are more likely to
   target older demographics.................1 2 3 5 6 7

Do you have comments concerning these ten
statements, or any other important issues relating to
your news coverage?

What attributes would the "ideal" TV news anchor
team possess?

This section asks for your attitudes toward older people.

Q-2 Do you agree or disagree with the following statements? Please do not skip any items. Circle your answer for each. (1=strongly disagree, 7=strongly agree)

1 A nice residential neighborhood has
a number of elderly living in it.......1 2 3 5 6 7

2 Most elderly would work as
as long possible rather than
be dependent..1 2 3 5 6 7

3 If the elderly expect to be liked,
they should eliminate
their irritating faults...........................1 2 3 5 6 7

4 It is foolish to claim that
wisdom comes with old age.............1 2 3 5 6 7

5 It would be better if most elderly
lived in residential units
that also housed younger people....1 2 3 5 6 7

6 Most elderly seem to be quite
clean in their personal
appearance...1 2 3 5 6 7

7 In general most elderly are alike....1 2 3 5 6 7

8 Most elderly make one feel ill at
ease...1 2 3 5 6 7

9 Most elderly bore others by talking
   about the "good old days"................1 2 3 5 6 7

10 Most elderly are cheerful,
   agreeable, and good humored.........1 2 3 5 6 7

11 Most elderly are as easy to
   understand as younger people........1 2 3 5 6 7

12 Most elderly complain about the
   behavior of the younger
   generation...1 2 3 5 6 7

13 Most elderly can adjust when the
   situation demands it...........................1 2 3 5 6 7

14 Most elderly need no more love and
   reassurance than anyone else...........1 2 3 5 6 7

15 Most elderly spend too much time
   prying into the affairs of others......1 2 3 5 6 7

16 Most elderly keep a clean home....1 2 3 5 6 7

17 The elderly have too much power in
   business and politics...........................1 2 3 5 6 7

18 Most elderly would quit work as
   soon as pensions can support
   them...1 2 3 5 6 7

19 The elderly have the same faults
   as anybody else....................................1 2 3 5 6 7

20 People grow wiser with the coming
   of old age...1 2 3 5 6 7

21 It would be better if most elderly
lived in residential units with
people their own age...........................1 2 3 5 6 7

22 Most elderly should be more
concerned with their appearance....1 2 3 5 6 7

23 Most elderly are very different
from one another.................................1 2 3 5 6 7

24 Most elderly are very relaxing
to be with...1 2 3 5 6 7

25 The elderly's accounts of their
past experiences are interesting.......1 2 3 5 6 7

26 Most elderly are irritable,
grouchy, and unpleasant..................1 2 3 5 6 7

27 The elderly seldom complain about
the behavior of younger people......1 2 3 5 6 7

28 It's hard to figure out what makes
the elderly tick..................................1 2 3 5 6 7

29 Most elderly are set in
their ways..1 2 3 5 6 7

30 Most elderly make excessive demands
for love and reassurance..................1 2 3 5 6 7

31 Most elderly respect the privacy
of others...1 2 3 5 6 7

32 Most elderly let their homes
become shabby and unattractive.....1 2 3 5 6 7

Television News and the Elderly

33 The elderly have too little power
   in business and politics......................1 2 3 5 6 7

34 A nice residential neighborhood has
   few elderly living in it......................1 2 3 5 6 7

        The next sections ask for your views on the
importance of certain news stories, and the
composition of your news audience.

Q-3 Do you agree or disagree that the following
stories would be <u>very</u> important to your local
television news audience? Please do not skip any
items. Circle your answer for each. (1=strongly
disagree, 7=strongly agree)

1 Advancement in cataract surgery...1 2 3 5 6 7

2 Doctor-assisted suicides.....................1 2 3 5 6 7

3 Proposed Social Security cuts..........1 2 3 5 6 7

4 Funding of local public education..1 2 3 5 6 7

5 Nursing home abuses.......................1 2 3 5 6 7

6 Local property tax squabble............1 2 3 5 6 7

7 City-enforced curfews for teens......1 2 3 5 6 7

8 Lower mortgage rates.......................1 2 3 5 6 7

9 Low interest rates on investments..1 2 3 5 6 7

10 Age discrimination lawsuits...........1 2 3 5 6 7

Q-4 Do you agree or disagree with the following statements? Please do not skip any items. Circle your answer for each.

Our station is interested in attracting viewers of all ages for our local newscasts.

Agree   Disagree

Older viewers are an important segment of our local news audience.

Agree   Disagree

Our local newscasts are targeted at older viewers.

Agree   Disagree

The last section asks for demographic information.

Q-5 In what year were you born?_____.

Q-6 At what age will you retire from full-time work?_____.

Q-7 In what year did you begin working in broadcasting or media?_____.

Q-8 In what year did you begin working for this station?_____.

Q-9 Occupation (circle one)
     1 general manager
     2 news director

Q-10 Gender (circle one)
        1 female
        2 male

Q-11 Which is the highest level of education that you
have completed? (circle one)
        1 attended and/or completed high school
        2 some college
        3 completed college
        4 some graduate work
        5 advanced degree

Q-12 If you attended college, what was your major
field?
        1 mass communication
        2 journalism
        3 speech
        4 broadcasting
        5 business
        6 liberal arts other than mass communication
           other-specify_____.

Q-13 Which of the following best describes your racial
or ethnic identification?
        1 black
        2 asian
        3 hispanic
        4 native American
        5 white
           other-specify_____.

Q-14 If living, what is the age of your father?_____.

Q-15 If living, what is the age of your mother?_____.

Q-16 What is your marital status?
1 never married
2 married
3 divorced
4 separated
5 widowed

Q-17 What is the age of your spouse?_____.

Q-18 How many children do you have?_____.

Q-19 Do you have children in the following age categories?

0-17	Yes	No
18-34	Yes	No
35-49	Yes	No
50-64	Yes	No
65+	Yes	No

Q-20 What was your total household gross annual income last year?
1 below $10,000
2 between $10,000 and $20,000
3 between $20,000 and $35,000
4 between $35,000 and $50,000
5 over $50,000

Q-21 What was your individual gross annual income last year?
1 below $10,000
2 between $10,000 and $20,000
3 between $20,000 and $35,000
4 between $35,000 and $50,000
5 over $50,000

Do you have any other comments on topics raised in this survey? Thank you for your participation.

References

Adams, W. C. (1978). Local public affairs content of TV news. *Journalism Quarterly, 55*(4), 690-695.

Ajzen, I., & Fishbein, M. (1980). *Understanding attitudes and predicting behavior.* Englewood Cliffs, NJ: Prentice-Hall.

Aronoff, C. (1974). Old age in prime time. *Journal of Communication, 24,* 86-87.

Atchley, R. C. (1991). *Social forces and aging.* Belmont, CA: Wadsworth.

Atkin, C. K. (1976). Mass media and the aging. In H. J. Oyer & E. J. Oyer (Eds.), *Aging and communication,* (pp. 99-119). Baltimore, MD: University Park Press.

Atkins, T. V., Jenkins, M. C., & Perkins, M. H. (1990-1991). Portrayl of persons in television commercials age 50 and older. *Psychology: A Journal of Human Behavior, 27-28,* 30-37.

Auerback, D., & Levenson, R., Jr. (1977). Second impressions: attitude changes in college students toward the elderly. *The Gerontologist, 17,* 362-366.

Babbie, E. R. (1992). *The practice of social research.* (6th edition). Belmont, CA: Wadsworth.

Bagshaw, M., & Adams, M. (1985-1986). Nursing home nurses' attitudes, empathy, and ideologic orientation. *International Journal of Aging and Human Development, 22,* 235-246.

Barrow, G. M. (1989). *Aging, the individual, and society.* (4th edition). St. Paul, MN: West.

Barton, R. L. (1977). Soap operas provide meaningful communication for the elderly. *Feedback, 19,* 5-8.

Barton, R. L., & Schreiber, E. S. (1978). Media and aging: a critical review of an expanding field of communication research. *Central States Speech Journal, 29,* 173-186.

Bell, J. (1992). In search of a discourse on aging: the elderly on television. *The Gerontologist, 32*(3), 305-311.

Bishop, J. M., & Krause, D. R. (1984). Depictions of aging and old age on Saturday morning television. *The Gerontologist, 24*(1), 91-94.

Bliese, N. W. (1986). Media in the rocking chair: media uses and functions among the elderly. In G. Gumpert & R. Cathcart (Eds.), *Inter/media, interpersonal communication in a media world* (pp. 573-582). (3rd edition). New York: Oxford Press.

Bogart, L. (1980). Television news as entertainment. In P. H. Tannenbaum (Ed.), *The entertainment functions of television* (pp. 209-249). Hillsdale, NJ: Lawrence Erlbaum.

Bower, R. T. (1973). *Television and the public.*
New York: Holt, Rinehart and Winston.

Bower, R. T. (1985). *The changing television audience
in America.* New York: Columbia University
Press.

Bramlett-Soloman, S., & Wilson, V. (1989). Images of
the elderly in Life and Ebony, 1978-87.
Journalism Quarterly, 66, 185-188.

Broadcasting. (1987, March 30). Pp. 163-164.

Broadcasting & cable market place. (1993). New
Providence, NJ: R. R. Bowker.

Cable News Network. (November 12, 1993). *Love, sex
and romance after 50 - part 1.*

Carmichael, C. W. (1976). Communication and
gerontology: interfacing disciplines. *Journal of
the Western Speech Communication
Association, 40*(2), 121-129.

Carmichael, C. W., Botan, C. H., & Hawkins, R. (1988).
Human communication and the aging process.
Prospect Heights, IL: Waveland Press.

Cassata, M. B. (1985). *Television looks at aging.*
New York: Television Information Office.

Cassata, M. B., Anderson, P. A., & Skill, T. D. (1980).
The older adult in daytime serial drama.
Journal of Communication, 30(1), 48-49.

Cassata, M. B., Anderson, P. A., & Skill, T. D. (1983). Images of old age on daytime. In M. B. Cassata & T. D. Skill (Eds.), *Life on daytime television: tuning-in American serial drama* (pp. 37-44). Norwood, NJ: Ablex Publishing.

Cassata, M. B., & Irwin, B. (1989). Going for the gold: prime time's sexy seniors. *Media & Values, 45,* 12-14.

Chaffee, S. H., & Wilson, D. G. (1975). *Adult life cycle changes in mass media use.* Paper presented to the Association for Education in Journalism, Ottawa, Canada.

Chandler, J., Rachal, J., & Kazelskis, R. (1986). Attitudes of long-term care nursing personnel toward the elderly. *The Gerontologist, 26,* 551-555.

Clements, M. (December 12, 1993). What we say about aging. *Parade,* pp. 4-5.

Comstock, G. A., Chaffee, S., Katzman, N., McCombs, M., & Roberts, D. (1978). *Television and human behavior.* New York: Columbia University Press.

Coulson, D. C., & Macdonald, S. (1992). Television journalists' perceptions of group ownership and their stations' local news coverage. In S. Lacy, A. B. Sohn, & R. H. Giles (Eds.), *Readings in media management.* Columbia, SC: Association for Education in Journalism and Mass Communication.

Cumming, E., & Henry, W. E. (1961). *Growing old: the process of disengagement.* New York: Basic Books.

Dail, P. W. (1988). Prime-time television portrayals of older adults in the context of family life. *The Gerontologist, 28*(5), 700-706.

Danowski, J. (1975). *Informational aging: interpersonal and mass communication patterns at a retirement community.* Paper presented to the Gerontological Society, Louisville, KY.

Davis, R. H. (1971). Television and the older adult. *Journal of Broadcasting, 15,* 153-159.

Davis, R. H., & Davis, J. A. (1985). *TV's image of the elderly.* Lexington, MA: D.C. Heath.

Davis, R. H., & Edwards, A. E. (1975). *Television: a therapeutic tool for the aged.* Los Angeles: University of Southern California.

Davis, R. H., Edwards, A. E., Bartel, D. J., & Martin, D. (1976). Assessing television viewing behavior of older adults. *Journal of Broadcasting, 20*(1), 69-88.

Davis, R. H., & Kubey, R. W. (1982). Growing old on television and with television. In D. Pearl, L. Bouthilet, & J. Lazar (Eds.), *Television and behavior: ten years of scientific progress and implications for the eighties, volume II, technical reviews* (pp.201-208). Rockville, MD: National Institute of Mental Health.

Davis, R. H., & Westbrook, G. J. (1985). Television in
the lives of the elderly: attitudes and opinions.
Journal of Broadcasting & Electronic Media,
29(2), 209-214.

Dillman, D. A. (1979). *Mail and telephone surveys,
the total design method.* New York: John
Wiley & Sons.

Dimmick, J. W., McCain, T. A., & Bolton, W. T. (1979).
Media use and the life span. *American
Behavioral Scientist,* 23(1), 7-31.

Dominick, J. R., Wurtzel, A., & Lometti, G. (1975).
Television journalism vs. show business: a
content analysis of eyewitness news.
Journalism Quarterly, 52(2), 213-218.

Doolittle, J. C. (1979). News media use by older
adults. *Journalism Quarterly,* 56, 311-317, 345.

Downing, M. (1974). Heroine of the daytime serial.
Journal of Communication, 24, 130-137.

Dychtwald, K., & Flower, J. (1989). *Age wave: the
challenges and opportunities of an aging
America.* Los Angeles: Jeremy P. Tarcher, Inc.

Elderly population expanding. (1992, November 10).
Omaha World-Herald, p. 3.

Elliott, J. (1984). The daytime television drama
portrayal of older adults. *The Gerontologist,*
24(6), 628-633.

Epstein, E. J. (1973). *News from nowhere*. New York: Random House.

Fang, I. (1985). *Television news, radio news*. (4th edition). St. Paul, MN: Rada Press.

Fisher, D. H. (1977). *Growing old in America*. New York: Oxford University Press.

Francher, J. S. (1973). "It's the Pepsi generation..." Accelerated aging and the television commercial. *International Journal of Aging and Human Development, 4*(3), 245-255.

Friedan, B. (1993). *The fountain of age*. New York: Simon & Schuster.

Gans, H. J. (1968). *The uses of television and their educational implications*. New York: The Center for Urban Education.

Gans, H. J. (1979). *Deciding what's news*. New York: Pantheon Books.

Gantz, W., Gartenberg, H. M., & Rainbow, C. K. (1980). Approaching invisibility: the portrayal of the elderly in magazine advertisements. *Journal of Communication, 30*, 56-60.

Gerbner, G. (1969). Toward "cultural indicators": the analysis of mass mediated public message systems. In G. Gerbner (Ed.), *The analysis of communication content* (pp. 123-132). New York: Wiley.

102   *Television News and the Elderly*

Gerbner, G. (1993). *Women and minorities on
    television*. Research report. Philadelphia:
    University of Pennsylvania.

Gerbner, G., Gross, L., Signorielli, N., & Morgan, M.
    (1980). Aging with television: images on
    television drama and conceptions of social
    reality. *Journal of Communication, 30*(1),
    37-47.

Glick, I. O., & Levy, S. J. (1962). *Living with
    television*. Chicago, IL: Aldine Publishing
    Company.

Goedkoop, R. J. (1988). *Inside local television news*.
    Salem, WI: Sheffield Publishing.

Goodman, R. I. (1990). Television news viewing by
    older adults. *Journalism Quarterly, 67*(1),
    137-141.

Graney, M. J. (1975). Communication uses and the
    social activity constant. *Communication
    Research, 2*, 347-366.

Graney, M. J., & Graney, E. E. (1974). Communication
    activity substitutions in aging. *Journal of
    Communication, 24*, 88-96.

Greenberg, B. S., Korzenny, F., & Atkin, C. K. (1979).
    The portrayal of the aging. *Research on
    Aging, 1*(3), 319-334.

Grey Advertising, Inc. (1988). The who and how-to of
    the nifty 50-plus market. *Grey matter alert*.
    New York: Grey Advertising.

Harmon, M. D. (1989). *Featured persons in local television news*. Paper presented to the Association for Education in Journalism and Mass Communication, Washington, DC.

Head, S. W., Sterling, C. H., & Schofield, L. B. (1994). *Broadcasting in America, a survey of electronic media*. (7th edition). Boston: Houghton Mifflin.

Hellbusch, J. S. (1994). A survey of physicians' attitudes toward aging. *Gerontology and Geriatrics Education*, in press.

Hess, B. B. (1974) Stereotypes of the aged. *Journal of Communication, 24,* 76-85.

Hiemstra, R., Goodman, M., Middlemiss, M. A., Vosco, R., & Ziegler, N. (1983). How older persons are portrayed in television advertising: implications for educators. *Educational Gerontology, 9,* 111-122.

Hilt, M. L. (1992). Television news and elderly persons. *Psychological Reports, 71,* 123-126.

Horton, D., & Wohl, R. R. (1986). Mass communication and para-social interaction: observation on intimacy at a distance. In G. Gumpert & R. Cathcart (Eds.), *Inter/media, interpersonal communication in a media world* (pp.185-206). (3rd edition). New York: Oxford Press.

Hummert, M. L., Garstka, T. A., Bonnesen, J. L., & Strahm, S. (1993). *Attitude, age and typicality judgments of stereotypes of the elderly.* Paper presented to the 46th Scientific Meeting of the Gerontological Society, New Orleans, LA.

Iyengar, S., & Kinder, D. R. (1987). *News that matters.* Chicago, IL: University of Chicago Press.

Kent, K. E., & Rush, R. R. (1976). How communication behavior of older persons affects their public affairs knowledge. *Journalism Quarterly, 53*(1), 40-46.

Kogan, N. (1961). Attitudes toward old people: the development of a scale and examination of correlates. *Journal of Abnormal and Social Psychology, 62,* 44-54.

Kogan, R. (1992, August 14). Networks not following focus on older americans. *Omaha World Herald,* p. 45.

Korzenny, F., & Neuendorf, K. (1980). Television viewing and self-concept of the elderly. *Journal of Communication, 30*(1), 71-80.

Kremer, J. F. (1988). Effects of negative information about aging on attitudes. *Educational Gerontology, 14,* 69-80.

Kubey, R. W. (1981). Television and aging: past, present, and future. *The Gerontologist, 20*(1), 16-35.

Levine, G. F. (1986). Learned helplessness in local TV news. *Journalism Quarterly, 63*(1), 12-18, 23.

Levinson, R. (1973). From Olive Oyl to Sweet Polly Purebred: sex role stereotypes and televised cartoon. *Journal of Popular Culture, 9,* 561-572.

Lieberman, S., & McCray, J. (April 1994). Coming of age in the newsroom. *Quill, 82*(3), 33-34.

Lipschultz, J. H., & Hilt, M. L. (1992). *Political and social views of broadcast general managers and news directors in the United States.* Paper presented to the Association for Education in Journalism and Mass Communication, Montreal, Canada.

Lipschultz, J. H., & Hilt, M. L. (1993). First amendment vs. business orientations of broadcast general managers and news directors. *Journalism Quarterly, 70*(3), 518-527.

Louis Harris and Associates, Inc. (1975). *The myth and reality of aging in America.* Washington, DC: National Council on Aging.

Louis Harris and Associates, Inc. (1981). *Aging in the eighties: America in transition.* Washington, DC: National Council on Aging.

Lowenthal, M. F., & Boler, D. (1965). Voluntary vs. involuntary social withdrawal. *Journal of Gerontology, 20,* 363-371.

Mares, M. L., & Cantor, J. (1992). Elderly viewers'
    responses to televised portrayals of old age.
    Communication Research, 19(4), 459-478.

Markson, E., Pratt, F., & Taylor, S. (1989). Teaching
    gerontology to the business community:
    project older consumer. *Educational
    Gerontology, 15,* 285-295.

Merrill, J. M., Laux, L. F., Lorimor, R. J., Thornby, J. I.,
    & Vallbona, C. (1993). *Machiavellianism
    (MACH), social desirability (SD) and
    perception of success in treating the elderly
    (ASE).* Paper presented to the 46th Scientific
    Meeting of the Gerontological Society, New
    Orleans, LA.

Moss, M. S., & Lawton, M. P. (1982). Time budgets of
    older people: a window on lifestyles. *Journal
    of Gerontology, 37,* 115-123.

Murphy-Russell, S., Die, A. H., & Walker, J. L., Jr.
    (1986). Changing attitudes toward the elderly:
    the impact of three methods of attitude change.
    Educational Gerontology, 12, 241-251.

Nielsen estimates: national audience demographics
    report, November, 1974. *Nielsen '75.* Chicago,
    IL: A.C. Nielsen.

Northcott, H. (1975). Too young, too old--age in the
    world of television. *The Gerontologist, 15,*
    184-186.

Nussbaum, J. F., Thompson, T., & Robinson, J. D.
    (1989). *Communication and aging.* New York:
    Harper & Row.

Palmgreen, P., Wenner, L. A., & Rayburn, J. D., II.
(1980). Relations between gratifications sought
and obtained: a study of television news.
Communication Research, 7, 161-192.

Passuth, P. M., & Bengston, V. L. (1988). Sociological
theories of aging: current perspectives and
future directions. In J. E. Birren & V. L.
Bengston (Eds.), *Emergent theories of aging*
(pp. 333-355). New York: Springer Publishing.

Peale, B., & Harmon, M. (1991). *Television news
consultants: exploration of their effect on content.*
Paper presented to the Association for
Education in Journalism and Mass
Communication, Boston, MA.

Perse, E. M. (1990). Cultivation and involvement with
local television news. In N. Signorielli & M.
Morgan (Eds.), *Cultivation analysis* (pp. 51-69).
Newbury Park, CA: Sage.

Peterson, M. (1973). The visibility and image of old
people on television. *Journalism Quarterly,
50*(3), 569-573.

Pollack, R. F. (1989). Granny bashing: new myth
recasts elders as villains. *Media & Values, 45,*
2-4.

Powell, F. C., Thorson, J.A., Kara, G., & Uhl, H. S. M.
(1990). Stability of medical students' attitudes
toward aging and death. *The Journal of
Psychology, 124*(3), 339-342.

Powell, L. A., & Williamson, J. B. (1985). The mass
media and the aged. *Social Policy, 21*, 38-49.

Powers, M. H. (1992). *Saturday morning children's television and depictions of old age.* Unpublished master's thesis, University of Nebraska at Omaha.

Quarderer, J. M., & Stone, V. A. (April 1989a). NDs and GMs define news 'profitability'. *Communicator, 43*(4), 10-12.

Quarderer, J. M., & Stone, V. A. (May 1989b). NDs and GMs describe their managerial 'marriages.' *Communicator, 43*(5), 32-34.

Rahtz, D. R., Sirgy, M. J., & Meadow, H. L. (1989). The elderly audience: correlates of television orientation. *Journal of Advertising, 18*(3), 9-20.

Ramsdell, M. (1973). The trauma of TV's troubled soap families. *Family Coordinator, 22,* 299-304.

Reichert, M., & Baltes, M. M. (1993). *Helping behavior toward the elderly: an experimental analysis of the effect of expectations.* Paper presented to the 46th Scientific Meeting of the Gerontological Society, New Orleans, LA.

Roper Organization, Inc. (1989). *Public attitudes toward television and other media in a time of change.* (No. 14) New York: Television Information Office.

Rose, T., Coen, J. C., & Gatz, M. (1993). *Differences in therapist communication techniques when interviewing older and younger adults.* Paper presented to the 46th Scientific Meeting of the Gerontological Society, New Orleans, LA.

Rubin, A. M. (1982). Directions in television and aging research. *Journal of Broadcasting, 26*(2), 537-551.

Rubin, A. M. (1988). Mass media and aging. In C. W. Carmichael, C. H. Botan, & R. Hawkins (Eds.), *Human communication and the aging process* (pp. 155-165). Prospect Heights, IL: Waveland Press.

Rubin, A. M., & Rubin, R. B. (1981). Age, context and television use. *Journal of Broadcasting, 25*(1), 1-13.

Rubin, A. M., & Rubin, R. B. (1982a). Contextual age and television use. *Human Communication Research, 8*(3), 228-244.

Rubin, A. M., & Rubin, R. B. (1982b). Older persons' TV viewing patterns and motivations. *Communication Research, 9*(2), 287-313.

Rubin, A. M., Perse, E. M., & Powell, R. A. (1985). Loneliness, parasocial interaction, and local television news viewing. *Human Communication Research, 12*, 155-180.

Ryan, E. B., Boich, L. H., & Wiemann, J. A. (1993). *The social utility of using age stereotypes for conversational management.* Paper presented to the 46th Scientific Meeting of the Gerontological Society, New Orleans, LA.

Saltzman, J. (1979). How to manage TV news. *Human Behavior, 8*, 65-73.

Scales, A. M. (1996). Examining what older adults read and watch on TV. *Educational Gerontology, 22,* 215-227.

Schonfeld, R. (1983, September-October). Pop news, TV's growth industry. *Channels, 3,* 34-38.

Schramm, W. (1969). Aging and mass communication. In M. W. Riley, J. W. Riley, & M. E. Johnson (Eds.), *Aging and society, volume two: aging and the professions* (pp.352-375). New York: Russell Sage Found.

Schreiber, E. S., & Boyd, D. A. (1980). How the elderly perceive television commercials. *Journal of Communication, 30*(1), 61-70.

Shaw, M. E., & Wright, J. M. (1967). *Scales for the measurement of attitudes.* New York: McGraw-Hill.

Signorielli, N., & Gerbner, G. (1978). The image of the elderly in prime-time television drama. *Generations, 3,* 10-11.

Singletary, M. (1994). *Mass communication research.* New York: Longman.

Smith, C. (1988). News critics, newsworkers and local television news. *Journalism Quarterly, 65*(2), 341-346.

Steiner, G. A. (1963). *The people look at television.* New York: Knopf.

Stempel, G. H., III. (1988). Topic and story choice of five network newscasts. *Journalism Quarterly*, 65(3), 750-752.

Stone, V. A. (September 1988). News directors move for professional advancement. *Communicator*, 42(9), 16-18.

Swayne, E., & Greco, A. (1987). The portrayal of older Americans in television commercials. *Journal of Advertising*, 16(1), 47-54.

Tebbel, J. (1975). *Aging in America: implications for the mass media*. Washington, DC: National Council on Aging.

Thorson, J. A. (1975). *Variations in attitudes toward the aged held by selected groups in the southern United States*. Paper presented to the 10th International Congress of Gerontology, Jerusalem, Israel.

Thorson, J. A. (1995). *Aging in a changing society*. Belmont, CA: Wadsworth.

Thorson, J. A., & Perkins, M. L. (1980-1981). An examination of personality and demographic factors on attitudes toward old people. *International Journal of Aging and Human Development*, 12(2), 139-148.

U.S. Senate Special Committee on Aging. (1987). *Aging America: trends and projections*. Washington, D.C.: U.S. Government Printing Office.

Usdansky, M. L. (1992, November 10). "Nation of youth" growing long in the tooth. *USA Today*, p. 10A.

Wass, H., Almerico, G. M., Campbell, P. V., & Tatum, J. L. (1984). Presentation of the elderly in the Sunday news. *Educational Gerontology, 10*, 335-348.

Weaver, D., & Wilhoit, G. C. (1992). *The American journalist in the 1990s*. Arlington, VA: The Freedom Forum.

Wenner, L. A. (1976). Functional analysis of TV viewing for older adults. *Journal of Broadcasting, 20*(1), 77-88.

Wenner, L. A. (1984). Gratifications sought and obtained in program dependency: a study of network evening news programs and 60 Minutes. *Communication Research, 11*, 537-562.

Whitmore, R. V. (1995). *The portrayal of older adults in the New York Times and the Omaha World-Herald, 1982 and 1992*. Unpublished master's thesis, University of Nebraska at Omaha.

Wicks, R. H. (1989). Segmenting broadcast news audiences in the new media environment. *Journalism Quarterly, 66*(2), 383-390.

Wimmer, R. D., & Dominick, J. R. (1994). *Mass media research*. (4th edition). Belmont, CA: Wadsworth.

Wolfe, D. (1987). The ageless market. *American Demographics, 9*(7), 27-29, 55-56.

Wurtzel, A. (1992). *The changing landscape of network television.* Paper presented to the ABC television affiliate stations.

Young, T. J. (1979). Use of the media by older adults. *American Behavioral Scientist, 23*(1), 119-136.

Index